# THE SWEDEN SYNDROME

# THE SWEDEN SYNDROME

## HOW ELITES COMMIT NATIONAL SELF-DESTRUCTION

### KARL-OLOV ARNSTBERG

ARKTOS
LONDON 2025

# ΛRKTOS

Arktos.com  fb.com/Arktos  arktosmedia  arktosjournal

**ISBN**

978-1-917646-97-0 (Paperback)
978-1-917646-98-7 (Hardback)
978-1-917646-99-4 (Ebook)

**Editing**

Josh Neal

**Layout and Cover**

Tor Westman

# Contents

# Editor's Note

D R. Karl-Olov Arnstberg is well-known in his home country, not only for his important ethnological work, but also for his outspoken politics. For over a decade, he has written and spoken about the existential crisis posed to Swedish society by the elite scourge of multiculturalism, egalitarianism, and Third-World immigration. He has done so, I should add, at great personal and professional risk. But this should not come as a surprise; all who have answered the call and dared to challenge elite opinion have suffered for their courageousness in one way or another. This is especially true for those individuals, such as Dr. Arnstberg, who were ahead of the times. To speak of the political and cultural challenges posed by integrating disparate population groups into an advanced, homogeneous, technological society was not easy to do a decade ago. It was much more challenging in the decades immediately following the Second World War (when Dr. Arnstberg first began publishing his research on the non-assimilability of Sweden's Roma population).

But what was 'radical' ten years ago is all but mainstream now: a decade of Trumpism, while far from having vanquished progressive neoliberalism, has nevertheless transformed the cultural and political landscape across the globe and made previously taboo subjects (e.g., opposition to egalitarianism, remigration) not only palatable, but politically actionable.

By 'Trumpism' I simply mean the accumulated efforts of what we might call conservative revolutionaries. Some readers might recoil at the use of the word 'revolutionary,' for it may call to mind images of the Bolsheviks or the Jacobins. On the contrary, these conservative revolutionaries didn't massacre noblemen and farmers or burn down their civilisations. Rather, they set fire to the normal standards for political participation. Not beholden to the demands of donors and special interest groups, these conservative revolutionaries — outcasts from the university system, the media, and just about every other institution of formerly good standing — established a new standard by which people could think about and engage with the political process. More aggressive, more analytical, and more media savvy (in particular, *new media* savvy), what this generation of thinkers and activists accomplished effectively dragged Western conservatism out of the proverbial dark ages and into a new era of political competition.

The transformation wrought by these conservative insurgents has opened a new space for ambition, curiosity, and innovation, which is precisely what Dr. Arnstberg offers in this latest work. Capitalizing on this new intellectual climate, Arnstberg has broken new ground. While he does not ignore his ethnological training, the analysis presented in this work utilizes a variety of different perspectives, culminating in a multidisciplinary approach that seeks to understand the multicultural turn Sweden has taken since the dawn of the postwar era. In addition to his keen academic eye, Dr. Arnstberg also brings a wit and levity to *The Sweden Syndrome*, qualities which one does not often find in political treatises or cultural analyses.

Importantly — and perhaps this seems obvious to some readers — he brings a technical eye to the question of egalitarianism and mass immigration in the European context. Many in the Anglosphere (including myself) first began questioning the conventional progressive wisdom only after hearing horror stories occurring around the world, particularly in countries like England, France, Germany, and Sweden. Such stories regularly shocked the senses over a decade ago, their effects still lingering. In fact, it is not uncommon to hear nationalists and conservatives in Canada and the U.S. declare now that "Europe is finished." But all these stories were shared through gatekept outlets in the legacy media, not from honest brokers. As a result, they could only ever produce sensationalism and despair, not true understanding.

Arnstberg does not shy away from exploring the more gruesome consequences of Swedish multiculturalism; there are a few passages which detail truly horrific and senseless crimes committed against innocent Swedes. Having said this, he does not resort to hyperbole, either. What Arnstberg *does* provide is a measured and informed view of the social and political transformations which have made Sweden the country we know it as today. For non-Swedish readers around the world, Arnstberg has done a tremendous job of relaying just what has happened, and *still is happening,* to the Swedish people.

While Arnstberg is not the only academic in the arena, so to speak, I believe that *The Sweden Syndrome* will usher in a new era of Swedish conservative intellectualism.

JOSH NEAL

# Foreword
## by John Carter

WHILE RIDING a municipal bus in Uppsala, I had the opportunity to observe a group of high school students. In one seat were a few Swedish boys, of the bespectacled, well-behaved, and soft-spoken variety typical of Sweden's intermediate professional classes. In the seat next to them was a small group of Swedish girls. Behind the girls were some Arab boys, who were engaged in pulling the girls' hair and otherwise tormenting and teasing them, much to the girls' displeasure. In other circumstances this might have been an innocent, even light-hearted scene, and there was a part of me that was amused by the Arab boys' antics and the girls' protests, but the rigid posture of the Swedish lads, the way they carefully looked anywhere but at the Arab boys, gave the scene a tense, dark aura.

Here in microcosm was a holographic fragment of Sweden's peculiar sociological madness. The Swedish boys were clearly deeply uncomfortable with the way the Arab kids were treating what they could not but instinctively think of as their women; whether their discomfort was due to the Arab boys' discourteous behaviour, or due to displeasure at these foreigners getting the attention of girls the way boys have always done, the fact of their discontent was obvious. The lads radiated a desire to intervene, but their inaction turned their anger into something futile and pathetic.

These boys had been raised to be good feminists and anti-racists. Whether they personally bought into these ideologies was immaterial, for they certainly understood the consequences of transgressing them. As good feminists, the girls were meant to be able to take care of themselves. If they wanted help, they'd ask for it; moreover, they certainly weren't anyone's tribal property, so the Swedish boys had no standing to protect their women from foreigners. As to the Arabs, the Swedish boys were trapped in the double-bind of anti-racist multiculturalism, in which they must simultaneously ignore race and be acutely conscious of it: they must not think of the Arabs as members of a foreign and hostile tribe, but simply as Swedes just like themselves; yet at the same time, should they assert themselves against the Arab boys, they would certainly be harshly punished for this expression of racism.

For the girls' part, I had no doubt that they would have much preferred the Arab kids to stop. Their body language was not of the sort that teenage girls use when they're being teased by boys whose attention they are pleased to have. Yet they too were trapped by the anti-racist imperative to avoid offending New Swedes by any means necessary, while also being prevented from asking for the help of the Swedish boys because, after all, they had been raised to be strong, independent women. Possibly some part of them felt angry at the Swedish boys for not standing up for them.

As for the Arabs, neither the strictures of feminism nor those of anti-racism applied to them one bit, and they knew this quite well. Thus, they felt no compunctions about taking liberties with the girls. Doubtless any attempt to stop them would have been met with unabashed racial verbal abuse and quite possibly physical violence. From the point of view of the Arab boys, the Swedish girls were nothing but whores, and as for the Swedish boys — who were required by feminism to defer to the girls — well, they were obviously even lower than whores, contemptuous creatures of no account.

It is a particularly sick society that binds the hands of its own men in this fashion, that its women may be offered up in the name of sexual liberation and gender equality to foreign invaders whom that same society refuses to hold to the same standard, because to do so would be culturally insensitive.

Over my time in Sweden, I made several similar observations: broken glass on bus stops, which would be repaired only to be shattered the very next day; gangs of young Afghan men prowling the downtown, staring at the populace with a frankly predatory gaze; female friends who would whisper to me, under their breath and with the door closed, that they didn't dare go out at night unaccompanied; other girlfriends who stated forthrightly that they'd stopped wearing makeup and started deliberately dressing down in order to dissuade the attention of these immigrants; stories of racial bullying in the schools escalated to such a level that the parents had no choice but to transfer their white sons and daughters; ubiquitous gypsy women begging outside grocery stores or shoving their cups under your face when you sat on the terrace (the gypsies were a recent arrival, having flooded into the country when Romania joined the EU, and having quickly identified the gullible, good-hearted Swedes as easy marks).

The pace of Sweden's demographic change has been rapid. This was brought home to me somewhat viscerally when a landlord from whom I'd been renting a room returned home one evening, shock written on his face. He was something of a recluse and a misanthrope, a retired engineer who lived at the edge of Uppsala but spent most of his time in his rural cabin. We'd had a few good conversations, as unlike most Swedes he had no illusions about the ill effects of immigration. Nevertheless, it was all somewhat abstract to him. When he returned to the apartment that night, he had just been to the city centre for the first time in several years. He told me that he thought I'd been exaggerating, but now knew that I had not exaggerated one bit: the city was completely changed, there were Africans, Middle Easterners, and Afghans everywhere.

Meanwhile, the good Swedes I met at work or in social settings were resolutely blind to all of this, convinced that there was nothing to worry about, that there were no problems, and that anyone who said anything to the contrary was a sexist, a racist, an Islamophobe, and probably a Nazi. When I tentatively raised the subject with one, he proclaimed confidently that such thoughts were the short path to Auschwitz. Another conversation that stuck with me was with a colleague who had spent a year or so as a conscript in the Swedish military, an experience to which I could relate, having served a few years in the Canadian militia myself. The subject of bar brawls came up: for myself, I'd always enjoyed the sense that the boys from my platoon had my back and vice versa, and that any civilian who threw hands was starting a fight with all of us; he'd been in similar situations, but found the unreflective tribalism of it horrifying. I pointed out that there were good reasons of evolutionary psychology for this sort of pack instinct, and that tribes which lacked it tended to go extinct; he responded by saying that we'd evolved past such things. Later, he explained to me that he did not care at all whether there were no ethnic Swedes left in Sweden by the end of the twenty-first century, so long as the people living in Sweden continued to practice Swedish values of tolerance and so on.

How does a country come, in such a short period of time, to embrace its own annihilation with such enthusiastic abandon? In other European countries, you might point to a bad conscience over the legacy of slavery or empire, but the only people the Swedes ever conquered and enslaved were other Europeans. With the exception of the Saami in the far north, Sweden had been perfectly ethnically homogeneous, with no oppressed minorities because there were no minorities to oppress. Some Swedes would tell me that Sweden had to make amends for its neutrality in the Second World War, as though tiny Sweden declaring war on Nazi Germany would have made a lick of difference. Others, bizarrely, pointed to the possibility that a certain amount of Swedish iron might have been used to forge chains and manacles for Trans-Atlantic slave ships, based on nothing more than the fact that those were made of iron, and that iron was a fungible commodity, and it was therefore plausible that a certain fraction of Swedish iron was put to this use.

To me, such justifications seem like ex post facto attempts to rationalize the phenomenon. To the contrary, I suspect much of Sweden's ostentatious self-harm is explained by Sweden's somewhat inflated sense of its importance on the international stage, a belief encapsulated by the Swedish government's characterization of Sweden as a 'humanitarian superpower.' Swedes are fashion-conscious people with an aristocratic assumption that others are looking to them and taking their cues from them. Thus, for instance, when it comes to Net Zero policies, Swedes will happily agree that even if Sweden became completely carbon-neutral, it would not make any difference to the global anthropogenic carbon budget, which is dominated by countries such as China or India who could not possibly care less about 'climate change.' Nevertheless, they assume that the whole world is watching what Sweden does, and that therefore Sweden must set an example. The actual truth is that much of the world is only vaguely aware that Sweden exists: your average American has a hard time remembering the difference between Sweden and Switzerland, for instance, to say nothing of the Chinese, who assuredly do not give Sweden a moment's thought in their daily lives. An uncharitable interpretation of Sweden's self-description as a 'humanitarian superpower' is that they are jumping in front of a parade in order to pretend to lead it.

Another important factor is that Sweden is a consensus society. Swedes are much more reluctant to violate social consensus than assertive Americans, eccentric Anglos, or the argumentative French. Say the wrong thing on the wrong subject, and be quietly ostracized. Sweden's elites astutely use the educational system and the media to manage the social consensus on race, immigration, feminism, and so on, with the result that Swedes feel an intense emotional pressure to conform to these ideologies. To speak against them too strongly is to endanger not just one's social life but one's career.

That isn't to say that every Swede agrees with all of this suicidal insanity. Far from it. There's a vibrant political underground in Sweden: large and well-organized nationalist groups; a robust and highly critical commentary sphere of anonymous online dissidents; and a large and influential nationalist party in the form of the Sweden Democrats. Many Swedish men, in private, will admit that they revile the self-destructive left-liberal tyranny. For now, the establishment has been successful in keeping such men from power, but I do not know that this will remain the case indefinitely. In a consensus society there is always a quiet conversation taking place underneath the public conversation, consisting of whispered private remarks and things that are said by being left unsaid, the purpose of which is to continually test the consensus. When a consensus is reached that the consensus has changed, the new consensus rapidly displaces the old, bringing abrupt changes in governance, law, public policy, and social norms. In Sweden, that quiet conversation under the public conversation has been proceeding furiously, both in pace and in tenor, for many years now. Moreover, it can't be ignored that the wider Western world is quickly souring on multiculturalism, replacement migration, feminism, and the rest of the intersectional left-liberal ideology. Left-liberalism is no longer hegemonic, and ordinary Swedes will certainly be taking notice of that. As open-borders globalism becomes unfashionable, political elites who cling to it look ridiculous and out-of-touch, rather than trendy and chic.

Perhaps that prediction of eruptive political change in Sweden will be borne out in the near future; perhaps, though, things will simply continue to decay, and it will strike the reader of a decade or two hence as obscenely wrong. Time will tell. For now, Sweden remains in the grips of this madness.

The present work by Karl-Olov Arnstberg is a thorough, clinical description of the symptoms and etiology of what the author calls 'the Sweden syndrome.' Arnstberg summarizes the Sweden syndrome's characteristics as a combination of oikophobia, hierarchical inversion (i.e. preferring the worse to the better, the lower-performing to the higher, and so on), reality denial (the postmodern superstition that objective reality does not exist, and that subjective morality can be treated as objective: as he puts it, '*pathos* replaces *logos*'), and the collapse of distinctions and boundaries (e.g. men/women, self/other, us/them, etc.).

Arnstberg traces the historical process that converted Sweden from a nationalistic *Folkhemmet* which treated the country like a family into a multicultural administrative zone that perversely prides itself on privileging the foreigner over the native. He shows how these beliefs were introduced into Sweden's elite and propagated through the key educational, academic, legislative, judicial, and media sectors. He shows in gut-wrenching detail the consequences for ordinary Swedes: vicious gang-rapes; teenage boys forced to submit to having their mouths urinated in after being robbed; legal persecution, public defamation, and career destruction for complaining about it. He demonstrates how the legal system has been twisted to harshly punish native Swedes, while letting migrants off with a slap on the wrist. He explores the deleterious consequences of feminization for Sweden's institutions following capture by ideological feminists, and how the imposition of feminist dogma turns Sweden's men and women against one another, and against their own natures. He demonstrates how the disease expresses itself even at the level of national symbols, for instance with the castration of the Swedish military's heraldic lion.

For Arnstberg, the Sweden syndrome is not a mere academic exercise, but something that he has lived through. He was personally acquainted with some of the principals who drove the early debate on multiculturalism. As a professor of ethnology at Stockholm University, he had both a front-row seat to the deepening psychosis of academia, alongside mastery of the conceptual toolset necessary to document and analyze the degenerative process. Finally, as an outspoken critic of the government's immigration policies, Arnstberg has personally experienced the regime's tactics of cancellation and defamation face-on.

The book is called *The Sweden Syndrome*, but the broad stokes of the disease that Arnstberg describes can be seen in practically every Western country. Sweden is not unique in this regard. However, Sweden presents an exemplary case study due to the rapidity with which it succumbed and the thoroughness with which the symptoms presented themselves. No matter what country you live in, you'll likely recognize the symptoms Arnstberg describes.

Arnstberg's concise analysis of this complex mass psychosis is a service not only to the present, but to future generations. While, as Arnstberg notes, we do not yet have either a vaccine or a cure, the first step to treating an illness is recognizing and describing it.

There are reasons to be hopeful that the fever is breaking. Since this book was written in 2022, the Sweden Democrats have become the second-largest party in the Riksdag and therefore too big to ignore. Thus, they have finally broken through the long-standing *cordon sanitaire* with which they were isolated from any meaningful policy influence, entering into the government as part of the so-called Tidö Agreement coalition with the other right-leaning parties (the Moderate Party, the Christian Democrat Party, and the Liberal Party). Meanwhile, the Swedish government has started experimenting with offers of lump-sum financial compensation to induce migrants to leave the country. These are small, tentative steps towards sanity. The Tidö coalition is an awkward one, particularly for the Liberals, and the centre-right parties have faced furious condemnation from both domestic media and their European counterparts abroad; while the Sweden Democrats are the largest party in the coalition (and the second-largest in the Riksdag), neither the prime minister nor any senior government ministers are drawn from the party. As to the remigration efforts, these have been completely unsuccessful, with only a few hundred accepting the government's bribe to leave, as compared to the million-plus who ultimately need to be removed. Nevertheless, these are small steps in the right direction, and mark the first reversals of left-liberal multicultural globalism in decades.

JOHN CARTER
Canada
November 23rd, 2025

.

# Preface

M ORE THAN a decade ago, I retired from my position as professor of ethnology at Stockholm University. Since then, I have written and edited about a dozen books on the consequences of mass immigration, 'wokeness' and political correctness, dishonest media, the feminisation of Sweden, the pundits' cancel culture, as well as the political class's very expensive ambition to remake Sweden into the planet's leading humanitarian superpower.

Unsurprisingly, I had to pay for my disloyalty. Journalists are herd animals, and when they get a lead on their prey, the drive is merciless. In a media frenzy, of course, it's best to be first — to get the scoop — but the most important thing is not to be last, not to break the news when the prey is already down and the hunt is over. The hunt often resumes when the opportunity arises to pounce on the victim again, which may be years later. The victim of a media smear campaign is made an outcast for most of the rest of his life.

As in war, truth is the first casualty. No one really has the time necessary for uncovering the truth of what really happened. Everyone is in agreement, and the event is presented in a similar way in all the places it is mentioned. The media have a monopoly on all the news material that is easily accessible and are therefore able to repackage the message so that it becomes impossible to penetrate.

This situation with the media can be explained by what French sociologist Pierre Bourdieu, in the mid-1990s, called *'fast thinkers.'* Bourdieu coined this phrase to convey a certain warning: when you are in a hurry, you can't think. The media are not analytical but *catalytic* — the main thing is to inflate the event so that it is optimally marketable.

What dissidents who have been subjected to mockery have in common is that they are either little known or completely unknown, and they have been affected because — and this is crucial — they have exposed institutionalised lies. In other words, what they have put out in public has been factual, or at least well-founded opinion. They have given words to 'the forbidden,' and the media's drive has been aimed not only at harming and silencing them, but also at showing other citizens that this is how bad it can get if you are disloyal and choose to blow the whistle on public lies.

Swedish media works to transform the perfectly correct claim that multiculturalism is a risky political commitment — one that generates social conflict — into a heretical act of racism, whereupon the person issuing the warning is called a racist (which in turn makes him every man's prey). It is almost never possible for the declared outcast to respond to the criticism or dispute the media's version. The person who responds to the criticism creates a new story, and that just adds fuel to the flames. The campaign spreads like wildfire, not only in all mainstream media, but also on social media.

Journalists don't see the smear campaign as an agitation but as doing their job. They work to create opinion and try to lead people in the direction they themselves have decided is the right one. The journalists do it of their own volition, and are prosecutors as well as judges. Targets are convicted without the slightest need for proof. The person who is exposed has no chance.

In Swedish, we speak of '*the opinion corridor*' to designate a narrow place where only those with the morally correct opinions have the right to stay. I was kicked out. Moreover, the gates to the academic monkey gym were also shut on me. I lost some dear friends. Even my wife left me. In me she saw the right-wing extremist I neither was then nor have since become.

Since then, I have made new and more interesting friends. Some of them, like me, have lost their right to stay in the opinion corridor. Others never even tried to be admitted.

A few of my old friends remained loyal and praised me for my courage. However, it was never a matter of courage; I'm probably lacking the tactical proficiency that is a prerequisite for hypocrisy. To me, it was an obvious obligation to write as truthfully as I could about the strange death of Sweden, to reference *The Strange Death of Europe*, a bestseller on the same theme written in 2017 by the British journalist and political commentator Douglas Murray.

In my research, I twisted and turned through issues, behaviours, and events, without realising that they were all pieces of the same puzzle. Sure, I understood how many of them were related to each other, but then I suddenly saw how they formed a pattern — all of them! What prompted me to write *The Sweden Syndrome* was the opportunity to finally put all these pieces together.[1]

Some readers may now react with an "Aha! At last, he has understood that it is one big conspiracy, and that the Illuminati, the Jews, the oligarchs, the global corporations, George Soros's Open Society Foundation, the Bilderbergers, the Rockefellers, the Pope, and Klaus Schwab of the World Economic Forum are behind it!"

Conspiracy theories come in a wide variety, from straw men to highly credible and well-documented ones, hushed up in public. What they have in common is the longing to understand why the West has fallen prey to what seems to be sheer madness. The conspiracy theorists say: "We no longer trust you. We are convinced that you are lying, deceitful, and malicious." Conspiracy theories, threats, and hatred all result from the lousy way those in power do their job. What goes around comes around.

It may well be true that within these speculations about underlying forces, there lie crucial explanations. However, I do not have

---

1 The Swedish edition was published in 2022: *Sverigesyndromet* (Debattförlaget).

the knowledge, contacts, or research tools that would enable me to uncover these conspiracies. Frankly, I do not need them. I apply the principle known as *Occam's razor*. One should not seek to "over-explain" the observations that one makes. This doesn't mean that I believe that what I cannot see doesn't exist. What occurs on the public stage rarely matches what goes on behind the scenes.

Since the end of the Second World War, the West has been dominated by two political fantasies: the left's vision of an egalitarian multicultural society, and the right's vision of a functioning globalism — a world where nations have been replaced by supra-national and trans-national organisations. Particularly since the turn of the millennium, these two opposing political forces have pulled in the same direction. The political right and the political left, albeit for different reasons, have been striving for the same future: a multicultural world without nations. For the right, it is a world in which capital and labour can flow freely; for the left, it is a world where national borders no longer prevent the global underclass from seeking a better life.

As I write this, there is a war going on in Ukraine. Faced with the risk of a Russian victory and the demise of Ukrainian statehood, many Ukrainians are prepared for the ultimate sacrifice. Now, in Sweden too, there is a rapidly growing realisation of the value of nationhood.

I wonder: what kind of Sweden is to be defended? Due to the mass immigration that places Sweden in a European league of its own, the welfare state has been largely dismantled. Violent gang crime is exploding; the police are understaffed and the justice system overburdened; the prisons are overcrowded; unemployment and welfare dependency among migrants from Africa and the Middle East is alarmingly high. One in 20 Swedes is on a waiting list for medical treatment, and almost half of them have waited more than the government-mandated 90-day maximum wait. If you start to add up the misery, the list could be almost as long as you like.

Among those who have provided me with invaluable help, I wish to mention four (all of whom happen to be journalists): Julia Caesar, Pelle Neroth, Gunnar Sandelin, and Trond Sefastsson. I would also like to thank readers whose names I cannot tell you, for that would be the kiss of death.

KARL-OLOV ARNSTBERG
Koh Lanta
November 2024

# Describing the Disease

THE SWEDEN SYNDROME is an identity-based social psychosis, an illness that takes the form of cultural self-harm. It is predominately found in Western countries. The worst affected are the 14% of the world's population who live in what we call 'liberal democracies'. Occasional outbreaks occur in other territories, but there the contagion rate is considerably lower or non-existent.

Among the infected, the capacity for reality testing is severely impaired; they claim that reality is a social construct and advocate for a linguistically and normatively imaginary world to which only 'the good ones' have access. What reality *should* look like takes precedence over what meets our senses. The distinction between fact and fiction — between right and wrong — is relativised. For the infected, empirical observations and well-founded perceptions also appear as opinions. One consequence of this is that what matters is not what is said, but who says it. The opinions of certain important people are particularly valuable, no matter how ill-founded they may be. The disease is highly contagious, and those citizens who have the capacity to build up an intellectualised view of reality are more likely to be infected.

Affected individuals and groups perceive their own Western communities, especially those of their men, as the oppressors of humanity. Members of other communities (which in Sweden are national minorities, ethnic groups, cultures and religions) are understood as victims. This also applies to perpetrators of various kinds. Supporters of the Sweden syndrome explain their destructive behaviour as due

to society failing to educate them into empathetic and good individuals. As a result, interest is focused on helping the wrongdoers, instead
of — as is normal for healthy people — helping the victims of crime.

Explanations for crime, violence, and other destructive actions
are brought back to the oppressors. In particular, white men, with
their cynical, capitalist, patriarchal and exploitative social ideals,
are blamed for various shortcomings. This is also true of relations
between men and women; the latter are axiomatically perceived as
oppressed by men. This perception is bolstered by notions of egalitarianism and multicultural superiority (the infected themselves fail
to perceive the transparent contradiction of such).

Those groups to whom representatives of the Sweden syndrome
assign victim status are usually considered incapable of discriminating or committing other destructive acts, and if they do, it is always
someone else's fault (usually society's).

The infected person has an individualised view of humanity and
sees those who distinguish differences between different groups, such
as between men and women, as evil. They are described in all too familiar derogatory terms like Nazi, racist, xenophobe, misogynist, etc.

The infected clamour for a language that makes no distinction
between people. For example, in Swedish, they call both men and
women *hen* rather than *han* (him) or *hon* (her). One of the surest
symptoms is that the infected emphasise the importance of not dis-
tinguishing between *we* and *them*. Those who do so are deemed racists or Nazis.

Those affected have little or no awareness of the disease; they see
themselves as good and describe healthy people as evil and morally
defective. Nations that prioritise their own populations and defend
their people against mass immigration — such as Hungary, the Czech
Republic, Australia, and Switzerland — are criticised by those suffering from Sweden syndrome. Politicians in these countries are considered undemocratic because, by protecting their borders, they do not
want to "take responsibility" for the world's refugee situation.

When those affected by this psychosis are criticised for not prioritising the interests of their own communities, they call their opponents fact-resistant, xenophobic, and right-wing extremists. They do so in spite of the fact that they are unable to defend their emotionally driven views with rational arguments. The infected see themselves as a balancing counter-movement to save all the world's people from the evil and fundamentally racist white culture.

The sick are prone to feeling disgraced. This has led to demands for trigger warnings and safe spaces, particularly in higher education settings. Any lecturer who intends to say something that may be perceived as offensive is expected to give advance warning of what is to come (safe spaces refer to the need for environments where those who are ill can avoid being criticised or questioned for their habitually extreme views).

Since the recognition of illness is tantamount to recovery, all criticism is fought on the principle of "when arguments are weak, raise your voice and look angry." Those who oppose the Sweden syndrome are sadly at the mercy of the infected, placed by them on a right-left political scale where any criticism that threatens to change the perception of reality is classified as right-wing. In more benign cases, they are labelled as 'populists' (also meant as a derogatory term). The sufferers do not apply the same politically biased scale of values to themselves. They consider themselves to be the bearers of an objective social morality.

For those affected by the Sweden syndrome, the world is populated by bad and good people. The bad must be fought on all fronts, which means that only the good can be granted access to the public arena. The Sweden syndrome is a socially destructive disease in which the infected do not understand that, in the name of humanism and empathy, they are eroding Western civilisation. The most seriously ill advocate social suicide, but without understanding it themselves.

## Symptoms

- Inability to prioritise the interests of one's own community
- Pathologically elevated empathy with minorities and out-groups
- Addiction to 'goodness'
- Pathos replaces Logos
- Fact-resistance
- Equality-centered feminism
- Race denialism
- A distorted sense of reality
- Language censorship
- Loyalty to the elite

## Dogmas

- Mass migration is profitable
- All people have equal value
- Multiculturalism is enriching
- Oppression is structural
- The *tabula rasa* (blank slate) is an ontological fact
- Gender is a social construct

## Focus of Interest

- Anti-racism
- Globalism

- Anti-nationalism
- Feminism
- Normative action
- Climate and environmental issues
- Human rights

## High-Risk Groups

- Journalists
- Politicians
- Women(especially young women)
- LGBTQ+ people
- Opinion leaders
- Teachers
- Writers, artists, musicians and other cultural actors
- Stand-up comedians
- University graduates (especially in the humanities and social sciences)
- Behavioural scientists (especially psychologists)
- Public officials

## Spreaders of Infection

- Expo (an anti-racist think tank)
- The morning paper *Dagens Nyheter*
- The tabloid *Aftonbladet*

- The Swedish Writers' Union
- Universities and high schools
- Political youth associations
- Media (especially cultural editorial offices)
- Trade union newspapers
- State broadcasting (especially Swedish television news reporting and Swedish Radio)
- Libraries and other cultural institutions

## Treatment and Consequences

A vaccine has not yet been synthesised. Worse still, therapies and medications have not proven to be very effective. Because the syndrome is identity-based and sufferers seek a short-term increase in well-being, they resist all types of treatment. In the long term, however, the socially constructed reality of the sufferers cannot defeat reality. Therefore, when the societal harms become apparent, the disease heals. Often, a lengthy period of aftercare is necessary, following the initial phases of shock and reorientation. The question is how much damage has already been done to the society by then. The prognosis is particularly poor for welfare societies. All signs indicate that they cannot survive more widespread outbreaks of the Sweden syndrome.

# Introduction

The *Stockholm syndrome*, as is well known, refers to the solidarity of abductee with the abductor, against the police who are supposed to free them. The *Sweden syndrome* means that a nation's ruling politicians and leading opinion-formers see their own country's interests, safety and their own people's well-being as a secondary issue. It is more important to take responsibility for "helping the world," i.e. to assume the role of a humanitarian superpower. The Sweden syndrome is characterised by progressive, egalitarian politicians benefitting from unending confidence in general elections gifted to them by voters who have been led astray by the media. An example:

The police killing of George Floyd in May 2020 led to riots in Minnesota. In Sweden, too, thousands of young people turned out to demonstrate in Stockholm and Gothenburg, despite the ban on gatherings of more than 50 people due to the Covid-19 pandemic. It should be noted that Sweden lacks a history of racial conflict like the kind we see in America. Nor is there any comparable antagonism between Swedish police officers and black citizens. If the demonstration had been about Swedish elderly care during the Covid pandemic, where government incompetence resulted in the deaths of many citizens, then I would understand the youthful protests.

The above example applies to citizens. Here is an example that applies to politicians and journalists:

Elder fraud is something of a Roma speciality. When I was doing research for my book *Roma in Sweden* (Sw. *Romer i Sverige*, 2015), I talked to the outgoing head of a police force situated in a small town in southwestern Sweden. They specialised in crimes against the elderly. At the time, the force had eleven employees, eight of whom were police officers. The gentleman explained that if his department had fifty police officers instead of a mere eight, that they could have solved twice as many cases.

Seven years later, these crimes against the elderly continued in Sweden according to the same pattern. Just how many crimes occurred is unknown. Many elderly people who have been cheated are ashamed of it and do not report the crimes, but there are thousands every year. In February 2022 alone, the police received 769 reports of so-called power fraud, which is the legal term for this type of crime. (the average in 2021 was 73 reports per day!). Since ethnic registration is prohibited in Sweden, it is not possible to know to what extent the perpetrators are Roma, but I find it hard to believe that it is anything less than the majority of the perpetrators.

The outgoing head of this police force had never been in contact with any of the politicians actively spearheading the Roma cause. To me it was obvious that those politicians and journalists were wary of contacting the police group, as it would threaten their ideologically based perception of reality. For them, Roma are and will always be the victims, and they certainly do not want to be told otherwise.

Although the justice system knows that Roma are mainly responsible for these shameful crimes, it is taboo knowledge among politicians and the media alike. Those Roma from Romania and Bulgaria who do end up in court are often sentenced to deportation after serving their sentences, but since identities are not checked at Sweden's borders, these EU citizens can freely re-enter the country.

Free movement within the EU is so important that the Swedish people are forced to live in a country flooded with beggars.[1] The person most responsible for introducing the first wave of the invasion of beggars was Sweden's then EU commissioner, Cecilia Malmström. I

---

[1]    In the fall of 2022, Sweden has a conservative government that has promised to ban begging. Hopefully they'll succeed.

have never seen any serious criticism directed at her. On the contrary, she was (and still is) much admired for her competence and language skills.

&

The Sweden syndrome affects the welfare democracies of the West in particular. You might ask, why should this policy of national suicide be named after Sweden? The answer is that Sweden is the European country that has gone furthest in its ambition to become multicultural. Back in the 1960s, Sweden was still one of Europe's most ethnically homogeneous countries. Our national minorities were small and did not politically challenge the Swedish majority. Today, Sweden is recognized for having taken in the most immigrants per capita out of all the other European nations. Approximately 30% of those with Swedish citizenship were born in another country or are children of parents who were not born in Sweden. We should therefore set a warning example to the rest of the world: *See, this is how bad it can get!*

# From Popular Rule to Elite Rule

## David Schwarz and Jonas Widgren

IN MY reflections on Swedish political developments, I often return to 1975, the year in which the Social Democratic government tabled the bill in Parliament that made Sweden a multicultural country.

The proposal was the result of the political work of two people. The first was a Polish Jew, David Schwarz (1928–2008), who came to Sweden in 1950, after a stay in a sanatorium in Italy. After recovering from both typhus and tuberculosis, he began studying sociology at Stockholm University.

On 21 October 1964, David Schwarz wrote an article in the leading morning paper, *Dagens Nyheter*, in which he pointed out that the number of foreigners coming to Sweden was increasing rapidly. It was important that these immigrants should retain their cultural distinctiveness and that Sweden should become a "multicultural nation." This was the prelude to a whole series of articles in *Dagens Nyheter*. The series inspired debate in other newspapers as well. Between 1964 and 1968, David Schwarz initiated a total of twelve newspaper debates on the immigration issue, a remarkable feat considering that no other person initiated more than one debate on the immigration issue.[1]

---

1    M. Eckehart, *Hur Sverige blev en mångkultur* (Logik Förlag, 2007), p. 28.

In the 1970s, I had quite frequent contact with David Schwarz. I interviewed him several times and it was clear that the man who came to be seen as the "father of Swedish multiculturalism" was not a spokesman for any group, least of all Swedish Jews, who seemed quite concerned about his involvement. They did not want to be in the spotlight, although they most probably sympathised with the idea of a multicultural Sweden. Nor did David Schwarz have a particularly strong position in the scientific community. He had some well-known supporters, but there was no real collective behind him. The support he received for his ideas is probably best explained by the fact that the time was simply ripe for his ideas. The post-war social-democratic welfare edifice was largely complete, and it was time to look at what was being done in other countries. Besides, Sweden could do better than Germany did with its guest worker system. While Germany exploited people who had the misfortune to be born in countries where it was difficult to make a living, Sweden could open its doors and welcome them. They could live in Sweden. In other words, Swedish national pride was in full bloom — and ready to show hospitality.

It also mattered that David Schwarz was a firebrand and as stubborn as a mule. We both lived in the same quarter of Stockholm, and if I risked meeting him on the sidewalk, I was often tempted to cross to the other side. Otherwise, I would be caught up in half-hour conversations, which not infrequently resulted in my being persuaded to do something, such as write an article for his magazine *Identity & Minority*.

The second person was Jonas Widgren (1944–2004). He was a member of the radicalised young bourgeoisie who received their ideological education in the late 1960s and early 1970s, with refugee activism and protests against the Vietnam War. We also knew each other and hung out in the same circles, but we had no close contact. Politically, he put David Schwarz's ideas about a multicultural Sweden into practice.

Jonas Widgren had a cosmopolitan upbringing in Stockholm, Marseille and Geneva. In 1967, he married a woman from Croatia and added Serbo-Croatian to the other languages he mastered. Unlike the hard-left students at universities, Widgren wanted to realise his ideals within the system.

When it comes to determining who was more influential in transforming Sweden into a multicultural state — David Schwarz or Jonas Widgren — it is hard to say, but if I had to choose, I think Jonas Widgren was the more consequential of the two.[2]

Later in his career, David Schwarz would become openly critical of the immigration bureaucracy he helped initiate. In 1983, he wrote in the Swedish Immigration Service's magazine, *New in Sweden*, that he was horrified by the immigrant world he himself had helped build.

Like David Schwarz, Jonas Widgren also came to doubt multicultural politics, although in his case it was much later, after the turn of the millennium.[3] In 2004, he died, aged only 60.

## Implementation

It is not known precisely when Jonas Widgren joined the Social Democratic Party, though we can say for certain that he enjoyed an early career. Many have testified that Widgren not only had a pleasant manner, but was also very adept at navigating his ideas through the political landscape. Like others involved in immigration issues during this period, Widgren believed that the "old monolithic nation-state" would crumble due to increasing immigration.

---

2   The description of Jonas Widgren's work is based almost exclusively on the research of the Finnish-Swedish historian Mats Wickström, especially the as yet unpublished *"Huvudsekreteraren och mångkulturalismen. Jonas Widgren och 1975 års invandrar- och minoritetspolitik."*

3   Mats Wickström, "The Principal Secretary and Multiculturalism: Jonas Widgren and the Immigration and Minority Policy of 1975." http://www.academia.edu/25306942/Huvudsekreteraren_och_m%C3%A5ngkulturalismen_Jonas_Widgren_och_1975_%C3%A5rs_invandrar-_och_minoritetspolitik.

David Schwarz also became a Social Democrat to make his political ideas heard, though his efforts were met with some resistance.
Increasing migration raised the question about the necessity of restrictions. The focus of the discussion was on whether immigration
was good for Sweden or not.

For many Social Democrats, the idea of being anything other than
Swedish in Sweden was alien, and it was obvious to them that immigration policies should be geared towards assimilation. Concern for
immigrants and their adaptation, which was David Schwarz's heart's
desire, was peripheral. If the first generation of immigrants did not
become Swedes, their children and grandchildren would. That was
the case with the Estonians who fled to Sweden at the end of the war.

But David Schwarz didn't just face resistance; he was also supported by leading Social Democratic politicians, especially the future
Prime Minister Olof Palme, who had a multilingual upbringing and
was internationally minded. Olof Palme was in the government since
1963. In his New Year's address on the radio in 1965, he broke with the
tradition of addressing Swedes abroad, instead addressing foreigners
in Sweden and taking the opportunity to strike a blow for internationalism. Among other things, he said that immigrants should not
be forced to become just like Swedes: immigrants could become "different Swedes."[4]

From 1965 onwards, David Schwarz used the terms "multicultural society" and "many cultural society" interchangeably. When it
came to promoting multiculturalism, it was hardly surprising that
representatives of various minorities made themselves heard, but several prominent Swedes also supported cultural pluralism including

---

4    Mats Wickström, "The difference white ethnics made: The multiculturalist
     turn of Sweden in comparison to the cases of Canada and Denmark" in Heidi
     Vad Jønsson, Elizabeth Onasch, Saara Pellander & Mats Wickström (eds.),
     *Migrations and Welfare States: Policies, Discourses and Institutions*, NordWel
     Studies in Historical Welfare State Research 3 (Helsinki, 2013), p. 39.

Olof Palme's speechwriter Olle Svenning, who co-wrote with David Schwarz.

The media debate led to a parliamentary decision in 1968, which stated that immigrants should be able to live at the same standard as the native population. It was also stressed that immigrants should be given the opportunity to maintain contact with the language and culture of their home country.

In the same year, the government set up an inquiry to identify the problems faced by immigrants in Sweden and to report on measures to promote integration into Swedish society. The unfriendly and alienating concept of *foreigner* was replaced by a more affirmative term: *immigrant* (Sw. *Invandrare*) had a better connotation, because it was still synonymous with labour immigrants. A new Aliens Act was passed, and in 1969 the State Aliens Commission was replaced by the State Immigration Service. Many organisations and authorities were eager to play their part.

In politics, however, immigration was not a major issue. It may sound like a joke, but the committee set up in 1968 was in its first year of operation, going by the name the "Committee on the Registration of Incoming Mail").[5] If you read the terms of reference, you don't understand what a big change was going on.

The Immigration Inquiry worked for six years, between 1968 and 1974.[6] Its final report, "Immigrants and Minorities," laid the foundations for a multicultural ideology. A unanimous parliament adopted the immigration policy, which is still essentially in place today.

## Canada as a Role Model

In December 1971, Jonas Widgren visited Canada to learn about their new integration and minority policies. Canada's Prime Minister

5   Bengt Jacobsson, *Hur styr förvaltningen? Myt och verklighet kring departementens styrning av ämbetsverken* (Stockholm, 1984), p. 73.

6   The government's official investigations: SOU 1974:69.

Pierre Trudeau, the controversial and charismatic father of the Justin Trudeau, promoted multicultural ideology in the Canadian Parliament. It did not attract much attention and was almost a by-product of the ambition to resolve tensions between Quebec and English-speaking Canada. The background was a Ukrainian senator's call for cultural recognition of "the third element of Canadian society." It was a relatively large minority he represented. In simple terms, the scenario was that if the English-speaking and French-speaking populations were to be put on equal footing, then other minority groups should also receive the same political recognition. It was not a dramatic change anyway, as all the actors were Christian and Canadian citizens with the right to vote. It was, therefore, not a major injustice that needed to be corrected politically.

It should be added that Canada, as a settler society, lacked a strong national identity. It was also already a pluralistic society that was successful in integrating newcomers. In other words, the situation was not at all like that in Sweden, except in the sense that both countries were economically successful and that multiculturalism was generally perceived as a relatively unimportant but nevertheless sympathetic political reform.

## The Inevitable Multiculturalism

In Sweden, the concept of multiculturalism began to take hold in common parlance. For example, journalists at *Dagens Nyheter* wrote in eager approval of the forecast that by the year 2000, Sweden would be truly multicultural.

Advocates of a multicultural Sweden had an almost fatalistic view of the future; immigration would only accelerate, and Sweden would not be able to maintain its ethnic and cultural homogeneity. Schwarz predicted that by the mid-'80s, Sweden would be home to several million immigrants. Of these, he imagined, about half a million would be Catholic, while Muslims would make up about

100,000. Apart from the fact that the proportion between Muslims and Catholics was more likely to be the reverse, his overall prediction was not far off. Schwarz believed that this would be an immigration that Sweden, for various reasons, could not stop or even limit. What those reasons were, however, he did not specify.

## An Outdated Decision

It is worth pointing out once again that the immigration inquiry was not important. Nor was the decision to adopt a multicultural policy of significant import. Politicians expected immigrants to come mainly from the Nordic countries, especially Finland. Otherwise, it was obviously about Europe. The estimates foresaw about 10,000 immigrants per year. Sweden could easily cope with that; Sweden had good annual growth, negligible unemployment, low inflation, and its citizens were convinced that Sweden would continue to rank high in the world in terms of advanced technology, education, and work ethic. At this time, Asia was not yet competitive on the international stage. National self-esteem soared, though it was modestly restrained when it came to external pretensions. Sweden's future looked promising, to say the least.

Accepting and supporting an immigrant population that contributed to building Swedish welfare did not seem problematic.

By 1970, politicians still agreed that immigration was a profitable business. Nor was it difficult to understand that anyone born in Finland — the largest group of labour migrants — who wished to keep in touch with their former homeland and mother tongue, should be supported in doing so. Here it was not even a question of generosity, but rather of what seemed to be reasonable rights in a welfare society.

When Sweden became multicultural, owing to the political slogans of *equality, freedom of choice* and *cooperation*, the refugee issue was not in focus. Nor did Sweden have today's ambitions to be a humanitarian superpower. Most immigrants were northern European;

almost half of those who arrived in the early 1970s were Finns. Other groups came from southern Europe, i.e. Italy, Greece, and Yugoslavia.

At this time, Sweden slid into a recession. Significantly, politicians failed to correlate immigration policies with the economic situation. The jobs that had attracted so many non-Swedes were no longer available. While the 1970s were a breakthrough period, the 1980s were dominated by refugee and family immigration. Nordic immigration remained low. It could be said that Sweden's multicultural immigration policy, despite being the first in Europe, was already outdated by the time it had launched. The policy in place was essentially related to Nordic and European labour migration, which had largely ceased. The overall support among Swedish politicians for the multicultural project was therefore based on false premises.

## A Farewell to Popular Government

The fact that politicians did not bother to examine the consequences of this multicultural shift is hard to understand. In May 1972, Widgren brought his ideas on migration and integration to a wider audience in his book *Europe and the Immigration Question*. According to Widgren, it was in the interest of European countries to integrate immigrants rather than assimilate them. In Widgren's view, the indigenous population should also be persuaded "to respect them instead of vilifying them," otherwise the immigrants' discontent could even lead to "painful but necessary revolts."[7]

Although Widgren was an advocate of a multicultural society, the phrase "painful but necessary revolts" was not at all in keeping with the *People's Home* (Sw. *Folkhemmet*) that the Social Democrats promoted. It would not have been difficult to find out how multiculturalism worked in other countries, i.e. that ethnic groups do not mix at all into a harmonious or "enriching" whole. Rather, they usually practise endogamy, live in segregation, and often find themselves in

---

7    Jonas Widgren, *Europa och invandrarfrågan* (Stockholm, 1972), pp. 4–5.

conflict with each other as well as with the majority culture. This lack of alignment also applies to both journalists and Swedish researchers. Everyone applauded, even though there was plenty of research and experience in other countries which should have given the Swedish power elite cold feet.

Nor do I think politicians understood that "multiculturalism" was a paradigm shift that severed the ties between themselves and the voters they represented. The Social Democrats who came to power elected by the workers, i.e. the majority of Swedes, would in future re-present neither the interests of the workers nor the Swedes, but instead only the following abstraction: "the equal value of all people." The 1975 government's position was revolutionary: it amounted to a farewell to representative democracy.

## The Political Nobility

The first person to understand, albeit belatedly, what the politicians themselves did not understand was the Social Democratic journalist Anders Isaksson. He first dubbed this new political order the *Political Class* and then later the *Political Nobility*.[8]

In 1996, he wrote that party power had become as characteristic of our times as the royal power of the past. The ideal figure of democracy, the elected citizen, was becoming increasingly rare. Politics had become professionalised and was conducted by a political class that had turned the office of the elected representative into a profession and made the state its livelihood. He likened the political class to a modern aristocracy. It created its own labour market, its own career paths in government, and its own security system via publicly owned companies.

In the run-up to the 2002 elections, Anders Isaksson went on to publish a small book, *The Political Nobility* (Sw. *Den politiska adeln*), in which he described the Social Democrats' transformation from a

8    Anders Isaksson, *Per Albin 3: Partiledaren* (Stockholm, 1996).

political party carried forward by a popular movement into a network of political careerists who determined their own political terms. This network set its own salaries, fees, and benefits. A politicians' empire had replaced a citizens' empire.

This form of corruption had resurfaced even though the Constitution mandates that the state should be meritocratic, equal, and serve the interests of citizens, not politicians. Skill and merit were to be the only grounds for promotion.

One such example occurred in April 2017, when top Social Democratic politician Carin Jämtin left both the parliament and the post of Social Democrat party secretary. A month later, she was appointed as the new Director-General of Sweden's international development cooperation agency (SIDA), one of the Social Democrats' flagship institutions. Of Sweden's gigantic 50 billion SEK aid expenditure, 1% of the national budget, the lion's share was administered by SIDA. Carin Jämtin had not applied for the post and lacked the qualifications set by the government as a requirement for appointment. Although the government advertised the post, it did not appoint any of the 28 applicants, but instead waited until Jämtin resigned.

When Social Democrat Håkan Juholt was sacked as party chairman in 2017, he was appointed ambassador to Iceland without any diplomatic experience and without having applied for the post. Another example from September 2019 also demonstrates the point quite well. Labour Minister Ylva Johansson was rewarded for her long and faithful service with the well-paid position of Swedish EU Commissioner; her state secretary, who was dismissed at the same time, had her livelihood secured as Director General of the Mediation Institute.

In practice, the power of appointment means that the government continuously appoints heads of agencies and several other senior officials in the state, such as directors-general, governors, ambassadors, judges of the Supreme Court, superintendents, etc. However, the recruitment of lower officials is delegated to the agency itself. It is not known how strictly this prohibition is adhered to, but clearly it is less attractive for suitable persons of good merit to apply for a post in an authority where the highest posts are filled by political representatives, whose competence as well as merit are regarded as secondary issues. The appointing authority, despite the requirement for objectivity, has long been deeply politicised. A significant proportion of the most senior managers in government have come from a partisan background, often members of parliament, ministers or political officials for one of the parties in government. A strong preponderance of Social Democrats has historically characterised these appointments. In the 2000s, up to a quarter of government appointments to high office have been from partisan backgrounds.

As with previous governments, the power of appointment, this seam between politics and bureaucracy, was an important instrument for both rewarding loyal politicians and providing for their livelihoods upon leaving office.

Even today, Swedish political scientists and other researchers probably do not fully understand the consequences.

## Party Support

Traditionally, political parties were financed through membership fees. When the number of members declined and the parties grew, the parliament solved the problem by granting the parties state funding, a so-called party subsidy. In 1965, the parliament took the first decision on party subsidies and the following year the first subsidies were paid out to the parties.[9] This was no small amount of money. For the financial year 2021–22, the parliamentary parties were granted almost 168 million SEK. To this should be added the government office, that is, the experts and specialists hired by the government. Since the 1960s, the government has grown eightfold. It now employs around 5,000 people, of whom 500 work in the Ministry of Finance

---

9    The Government Offices Annual Report for 2021.

alone. At the time of writing, the annual budget is around a 10 billion SEK.[10]

With party funding, parliamentary parties cut themselves off from civil society and became part of the state instead. Party support professionalises politics by making it possible for parties to employ civil servants and purchase political services. The parties' representatives thus become increasingly alike each other. All the economists who have worked in government, and on whose analyses the cabinet bases its policies, have the same educational background. They have all studied (and in most cases obtained doctorates) at the same Swedish universities, and thus they have been schooled in the same national economic theories that are dominant at Swedish universities. In other words, they all partake in the same ideological prejudices.

With the advent of party funding, parties in practice do not need more members than are required to pursue policies. The parties function as foundations. They own themselves and appoint their own beneficiaries.

---

10   The Government Offices Annual Report for 2021.

# Equal Value?

## Value and Dignity

THE UN Declaration of Human Rights begins with the words "All human beings are born free and equal in dignity and rights." The wording harks back to philosopher Immanuel Kant's categorical imperative in which one should "act only in accordance with that maxim through which you can at the same time will that it becomes a universal law." Kant's formulation can in turn be traced back to the Golden Rule, which in its oldest known form can be linked to Confucius.

In Sweden, the declaration has been translated as "All human beings are born free and equal in value and rights." One wonders why they didn't translate it into the more correct "dignity" as they did into French (*dignité*) and German (*Würde*). Unlike value, dignity has a more unobjectionable meaning, namely that all people should be treated with basic respect.

This is one of Sweden's basic laws. It was adopted by the Swedish Parliament in 1974 and came into force on 1 January, 1975, at the same time as the parliament decided that Sweden would be the first country in Europe to become a multicultural society. Its introductory paragraph sets out the foundations of the constitution. The oft-quoted paragraph reads:

> All public power in Sweden emanates from the people. Swedish government is based on freedom of opinion and on universal and equal suffrage.

It is realised through a representative and parliamentary system of government and through municipal self-government.

This is followed by a list of rights and protections against discrimination. The first passage refers to respect for the equal value of all
human beings *and the freedom and dignity of the individual.* The
concept of dignity is thus included, but only with reference to the "individual human being." Above all, it introduces the concept of value,
which came to dominate. In the *Introduction to the Common Core
Values for Civil Servants*, commissioned by the Government and published by the Government Office in 2014, the preface already states:

> In government, we are obliged to act at all times on the basis of the con-
> stitutional principles of the equal value of all people, the rule of law and
> good service to citizens. This must be in the back of our minds, otherwise
> there is a risk that we as employees will forget who we are for when we are
> engulfed in internal processes.

Later in the preface, the concept of dignity is also cited, and it is made
clear that value and dignity have become interchangeable. These
concepts are not subjected to critical scrutiny, but are simply words
of honour. There is not even a suggestion that the concept of value
is problematic. However, there is a big difference between these concepts. Value is something that varies and turns man into a resource,
which is precisely what Kant wanted to avoid.

Human beings are not resources, but regardless of their position
in the social hierarchy, every human being has the right to dignity.
When abuse is committed, it is dignity and not worth that is des-
ecrated. If we reduce them to resources, we open the door to exploitation. Slaves are not treated with respect for their dignity but precisely
as resources. As a concept, migrant labour highlights the benefits that
workers may bring to Sweden, but refugees should certainly not be
seen as resources. They should be accorded their dignity, not judged
in terms of value.

The transfer of an economic term, like value, to the level of moral philosophy, where it cannot function, may have something to do with the Marxist labour theory of value, where the value of a product is determined not by demand, that is, what others may be willing to pay for it, but by the cost of production. In that case, value becomes absolute and not a relational concept. This notion contributed to the collapse of the Soviet Union. The ideologically based notion of an absolute economic value perhaps explains why, when it comes to the principle of the inviolability of human beings, only dignity has been confused with this economic term.

Why the concept of "dignity" of the UN Charter became the concept of value in its Swedish translation and thus took its place in the form of government is not clear. In any case, in a constitutional revision, the concept of the value of all equals should be removed from the form of government. Rights should be linked to the individual, not to culture, clan or pigmentation.

Since Sweden is a state and grants citizenship to some people but not to others, there is a formal distinction between human rights and civil rights. For human rights, it is enough to exist; there is no requirement to do anything in return. Civil rights, on the other hand, are acquired only as a citizen of a country, and citizenship carries not only rights, but also obligations. But this distinction seems to be increasingly blurred in Sweden. One phrase that recurs in the Swedish refugee debate is "Asylum is a human right!" The possibility of seeking asylum may be a right, but it is of course not a right to be granted asylum in a specific country.

## All Are Swedes

In multicultural Sweden, there must be no advantages to being Swedish, and no disadvantages to being of a different ethnicity. The multicultural state therefore abandons the policy that naturally puts

Swedes first. The state, political parties, politicians, and authorities are supremely ethnically neutral.

For the multicultural state, we are all the same kind of anonymous individuals, and privileging any group or category is classified as racism and thus is strictly forbidden. In the Swedish media, therefore, if they have Swedish citizenship, even Muslim IS fighters are referred to as Swedes. That Swedishness is irrelevant to them is never said. That would be exclusionary!

The claim that we are all equally worthy is so often invoked in Sweden that it can be considered the most important dogma of the Sweden syndrome. In practice, it concerns the relationship between Swedes and immigrants and should be interpreted as the more understandable: "It is important that immigrants do not become second-class citizens. We are all equally worthy" — which in turn can be interpreted as saying that since everyone has equal value, Swedes have no more right to Sweden than any other group. In Swedish political debate, equal value is usually followed by exclusionary statements such as "The Sweden Democrats do not believe that all people have equal value" and "He is the kind of person who does not believe in the equal value of all people." The dogma of equal value for all is also used as an argument for Swedish taxpayers to take financial responsibility for people to whom they are in no way related, including those who are illegally staying in the country and are called "undocumented migrants."

In a parliamentary debate a few years ago, we had a demonstration of this view when then Green Party's spokesperson Åsa Romson declared that she was provoked by those who claimed that you are not Swedish just because you have a different culture. She declared: "I think that everyone who rides the metro is Swedish." Jimmie Åkesson of the Sweden Democrats responded with a question, "Then, if I ride the subway in Tokyo, am I Japanese?" But even if he got the laughs, Åsa Romson's definition trumped ideologically. Anyone who makes him or herself the spokesperson for the ethnic definition of Swedishness risks being disgraced and is held to be morally dubious.

One of the paradoxes that follows in the wake of dogma is that those who do not believe in the equal worth of all people are thus shown to be less worthy than the "true believers"; another is that an immigrant who quickly learns Swedish, is well educated, and attractive on the labour market is no more worthy in the dominant political rhetoric than a criminal illiterate who is directly hostile to Sweden and fond of throwing stones at emergency vehicles.

The dogma of the equal value of all human beings makes us interchangeable with each other, which in turn is tantamount to saying that we are all worthless. No Swedish politician can say the logically correct thing, namely that only if we are different — hence differently "worthy" in different respects — do we possess intrinsic value.

The dogma of equal value for all is contradicted by all the words we have about value differentiation. In a market economy like the Swedish one, the principle of the different value of everything applies. Without the so-called value gap, i.e. that buyers and sellers value the same good differently, no transactions would take place. The buyer must judge that the good is worth more than the price and therefore be willing to give up the resource represented by the price, and the seller must consider that the good is worth less than the price and therefore be willing to give it up if he is paid for it. This shows that value is a relational concept. Something has a value of a certain magnitude for one person and a different value for another. Wage labour is a fundamental example of this.

In other words, an addition is needed: "equal value for whom and in what context?" For example, I don't think that criminals in the likes of young gangmembers who raise Sweden's murder statistics above those of all other European nations have the same value as my own sons. Neither does the state. Parents are obliged to value their own children more than those of others through the obligation to take responsibility for them (financially, legally, socially, emotionally, etc.), but not in the same way for the children of others. Spouses are obliged to guarantee their partners the same economic standard as themselves, but not the partners of others. Priorities in health care mean that if resources are only sufficient for one of two patients, then doctors are obliged to value the patient with a better prognosis and longer remaining life more highly than the patient with poorer chances. The principle of equal value for all, if taken seriously, would mean that priorities in health care should be replaced by lottery.

## Everyone is a Refugee

In legal terms, this equal value has been reflected in the section of the law dealing with *incitement to hatred*, which, after first dealing with anti-Semitism, has now been extended to cover "race, colour, national or ethnic origin, creed or sexual orientation." The meaning of the term 'hate speech' has also been broadened: no one may say anything contemptuous about anyone else, because we are all equally worthy.

This context also explains why politicians and journalists insist on equating all immigrants with the concept of *refugees*. The Swedish public has ended up in the absurd situation that refugees are "very much of equal value." One of Sweden's most notorious agency heads, Director-General Dan Eliasson, demonstrated this in a morning show on Swedish television in February 2016, when he expressed his empathy for the murderer of a young female treatment assistant at an institution for teenagers with social problems in western Sweden. He said he was heartbroken not only for the woman who had been killed and her relatives, but also for the young perpetrator: *What had he been through in his life? What was the trauma he carried with him? The refugee crisis showed how unfair life was in many parts of the world. We Swedes must try to help as best we can.*[1]

---

1    https://nyheteridag.se/de-kraver-rikspolischef-eliassons-avgang-efter-om-mande-ord-om-alexandras-mordare/.

At the time of this writing, Russia has invaded and is at war with Ukraine. Ukrainian men between the ages of 18 and 70 must stay and defend the country, but millions of women and children are free to emigrate. Sweden, too, is getting its fair share. When Swedes willingly open their homes to these "real" refugees, a media debate erupts, accusing those who discriminate against refugees of racism. Politicians remain silent, except for the occasional Sweden Democrat who says what most people think, but which is not allowed in multicultural Sweden: yes, there are differences—implying that the young men from Afghanistan, Syria and Africa granted asylum in Sweden are not the same kind of refugees as the Ukrainian women who hope their husbands survive the war and want nothing more than to return home again.

## As Credible as Virgin Birth

What about "the others"—those who are supposed to be just like us? Do they also think we are the same? Do they behave in the same manner as the rest of us? It is hardly a reasonable expectation that as soon as they take their sandals off at the airport, "newly arrived Swedes" will also put their sense of honour behind them, learn to control their impulses, rule out cousin marriage, and no longer care about concepts such as Sunni and Shia. There is as little reason to believe that these people will change their character, gender, or culture upon arrival at the airport, just as there is little reason to believe that Swedes will start beating their children when they go abroad just because that is the proper way to raise children in some other countries.

Taken out of context, the statement that all people are equal becomes meaningless; put into context, it works once in a while, but most of the time it becomes either wrong, unreasonable, or downright silly. It is about as plausible as virgin births or the idea that paradise grants 72 virgins to suicide bombers and other Muslim martyrs (what do the women get, 72 bachelors?). It is, moreover, a dogma that is rude — indeed, it is difficult to find a more apt and intelligible word — because its adherents obviously consider themselves of a better breed than we who point out the emperor's nakedness.

## Would Rather Be the Best

All human groupings are hierarchically ordered. Some people pretend not to be, but that is simply not true. Someone is always more in charge than others; someone has the highest rank; someone is the highest paid; someone has the most desirable privileges.

It is a universal human aspiration to want to be better than others, because the achiever is admired by his fellow human beings. We are as anxious to bask in the admiration of our fellows as we are to fear their contempt. The desire to outshine others can be seen in major, decisive events such as war, in beloved activities such as sports and sex, as well as, of course, in the drive to get rich. This desire is not only the basis of conquest and imperialism, but also the condition of creation, whether in great symphonies, paintings, novels, codes of ethics, or political systems.

I know quite a few people who strive to be the best at something, but not one who aims to be "as good" as everyone else. And if I need help from an expert, I don't look for someone who is "equally good" but rather I naturally want to engage whoever is the best.

If we then raise our eyes and ask about the achievements of mankind, it becomes an almost ridiculous goal. What are the seven wonders of the world about? Hardly about everything being equal. Are all these artists whose works we admire and who are paid enormous sums of money the result of a quest to be "equally good"? Is that what Pablo Picasso wanted to be? Rembrandt, Monet? And Alfred Nobel, when he instituted the Nobel Prize, surely he did not think it would go to someone who was "equally good" or "equally worthy."

Let's try out the idea that man concludes his ambition and competition. Instead, we work just as hard as we need to satisfy our basic needs. That's exactly what animals do. The philosopher Francis Fukuyama wrote in *The End of History and the Last Man* (1992) that if man reaches a society in which he has succeeded in abolishing injustice, his life will resemble that of the dog. A dog is content with a walk and to lie in the sun and sleep all day, provided it is fed, because it is not unhappy with what it is. It doesn't care that other dogs are better off, or that its career as a dog has stagnated, or that dogs are oppressed in some distant part of the world. This is a mind game — It's hard to imagine humans ever ending up there. What I want to illustrate is that "human equality" is harmful even as a norm.

## Different Value

Multicultural societies are divided into oppressor (Western, white, patriarchal) cultures and oppressed minority cultures. What gives the political elite legitimacy is that it stands on the side of the oppressed and fights the oppressors.

Now imagine that the multicultural state succeeds in its struggle and gets rid of the oppressors. Then only the oppressed are left, but when they are no longer oppressed, what are they? Now we are in a fantasy, and multicultural equality is the obvious answer. But it is wrong, because collective identities are formed in the first place not by the collectives praising their own excellence but by pointing out the inferiority of other collectives. In social psychological terms, "all identity formation is contrastive." Thus, these "many cultures" must dissolve themselves for equality to emerge. If this project succeeds, which it of course never will, it will not be a multicultural society but a totalitarian one.

No matter how we behave, we will never achieve the ideal multicultural society that our politicians — if they are to be believed — have already imagined. What is happening instead, and now we are no longer in the realm of fantasy, is that Sweden is advancing along the totalitarian axis. The soft totalitarian society we live in today can, of course, harden, and it will do so if the Swedish power elite holds on to the dogma of the equal value.

A multicultural society must, in practice, fight multiculturalism (which is undeniably paradoxical). Otherwise, competition and conflicts between cultures will arise — conflicts so serious that they may very well lead to civil war. Multicultural society is not an ideological weapon for but *against* all communities, and most of all against the ethnic community that constitutes a majority — in Sweden's case, the Swedes.

Our politicians and opinion leaders must build their knowledge of the world and their political goals on the understanding of the *different* value of people. It is not weakness that should rule, but strength. Furthermore, to ensure that strength does not become an enemy of the people, it must be controlled. This can never be done by enforced behaviour via value bases, quotas and 'equal outcomes.' The result will not be an *Equal-Worth Sweden*, but a *Totalitarian Sweden*.

# Enemy of the Good

## The Ideal Society

THE MOST crucial factor for the possibility of building an advanced welfare state concerns the prevention of antagonism and disagreements that foment beyond control. Homogeneity is the basis not only for trust between citizens, but also for citizens' trust in their politicians; the feeling that "we are all of the same kind." Another important condition is that the country's rulers nurture their leadership and do not expose the population to war, oppression, famine or any other form of nationwide distress. If the population is hard-working and frugal, as it was in the Sweden of my childhood, then the conditions are ideal.

Politicians who realize what good leadership is may be confident that they shall retain power. However, "the good" can clash with what is "the best" — which is the subject of this chapter.

## The Problematic Freedom of the Press

Journalists like to think of themselves as the fourth estate. The first power is the government, the second the parliament, the judiciary the third and the media the fourth, with the self-imposed task of scrutinising the other three. It is not difficult to understand why journalists are so fond of the concept of the fourth estate. It gives them not only an important social role, but also privileges:

- Freedom from the principle of publicity and transparency in editorial offices.

- Freedom of information, which gives citizens the right to provide the media with material.

- The protection of sources, which is part of the freedom of communication.

- The prohibition of public servants from investigating media sources.

One concern that dictatorships and democracies share is that they may turn the media class against themselves. Ideally, it is beneficial for the media to represent the interests of the people, and to expose or prevent abuses by those in power. The problem is that the media does not put the interests of citizens first. Either they represent the interests of the elite, or they have their own agenda altogether. It may sometimes be in the interests of the people, but more often it coincides with those in positions of political power. They themselves deny this and say they are engaged in free and independent journalism, though we know this to be untrue.

In dictatorships, freedom of the press and freedom of expression are not held to be preserved. After losing the first free elections in Russia in November 1917, Lenin immediately dissolved the Constituent Assembly and established the dictatorship of the proletariat. All rights and freedoms were abolished, including freedom of the press and the right to strike. Political parties were banned. In 1933, Hitler did much the same.

But even politically elected leaders can have problems with the media because they have their own agenda. The good (freedom of the press) becomes the enemy of the best (a policy voted for by the people). Politicians find it necessary to restrict or abolish freedom of the press because it prevents them from delivering what they promised citizens and won elections on the basis of; the media responds by calling them undemocratic tyrants, on the order of a Lenin, Stalin, or a Hitler. In substance, of course, this is wrong, but the media are fighting for both their freedom as well as their existence. The politicians' most important channel to their voters is the media, which grants them enormous power. Few democratically elected leaders dare to go against the media. The risk of losing that battle is too great. The media has also, particularly in the last decade, faced competition from social media, where politicians make electoral contacts without having to go through the media.

## Opinion Journalism

In Sweden in the early 1980s, the idea of completely non-partisan journalism took hold within the guild. There would be a difference between the political editorial board of the newspapers and the other newsrooms that would engage in objective reporting. It was not the ideologies of the parties but the journalist's own values that would rule the day. At the same time, journalism would be neutral on controversial issues.

It was brilliant, but, unfortunately, explanations of programme are one thing, while the everyday life of the media something else. The journalists went in the opposite direction. They were not content with the neutral role of mediator; increasingly, they became active participants in their various features. In studio interviews, they appeared as experts and commentators. They revelled in opinion journalism and interpreted the intentions and feelings of actors as well as the meaning and significance of the events. In more formal terms, it is possible to identify four types of control over the content and form of the media:

1) The traditions of media editors, a kind of silent culture that can be described as "it's in the walls."

2) Journalists' political preferences.

3) Edition sizes, viewing and listening figures. In addition, we are witnessing a form of "clickbait journalism" for the online media. The material should be so attractive that the commercial media profits. Public service broadcasters are subject to much the same conditions. They must continue to be attractive for the state to want to finance them. In short, the owners must be happy.

4) The state financed media and large newspaper houses are regularly presented as passive owners. They assure us that they do not interfere in editorial work. In a democratic country like Sweden, journalism is thought to be both independent and free. However, this is not the case. The owners control the journalistic content by appointing managers with the right values and the right political stances. One example is the evening paper *Aftonbladet*, which is 91% owned by Schibsted and only 9% by the United Unions (the Swedish TUC, LO). However, through an agreement with Schibsted, LO has the right to decide who will be the editor-in-chief of the editorial, opinion and culture sections. Another example is when, in 2013, Peter Wolodarski was given the job of editor-in-chief of *Dagens Nyheter* by the owners (Bonniers). His idea of how journalism at Sweden's largest morning newspaper should be shaped could hardly have come as a surprise to the owners. Upon taking over, Wolodarski said, "We will focus more on agenda-driven journalism," meaning that the media will no longer be content to report factually on "reality," but instead will filter and create it. In addition, they will concentrate on a few issues, so that media consumers understand that these topics are more important than others. Two issues have dominated *Dagens Nyheter* almost entirely politically since Wolodarski took office: the climate issue and the warfare against the Sweden Democrats by almost any means.

## Media Engineering

In the blogosphere, it is said that the Swedish Union of Journalists had a meeting on 21 March 1987. There, an approach to immigration issues was formulated called the *Little Saltsjöbad Agreement*. The content was, if not exactly secret, never intended to reach the public. It reads:

> As an independent journalist, you have to take into account the following recommendations:
>
> Preferably positively assess and reassess Swedish citizens of foreign origin, especially in the context of youth, sports and artistic activities.
>
> For events with a multicultural element, preferably interview and visually highlight participants of foreign origin.
>
> Over a period of five years, systematically reduce the negative impact that the designation of certain migrant groups in criminal activities may have on affected populations.

It is also claimed online that this agreement has been extended, after some minor changes, i.e. "affected populations" has been replaced by "ethnic groups."

No journalist has ever confirmed the existence of such an agreement. In any case, Swedish journalists are agreed on taking their share of the responsibility for keeping xenophobia in Sweden at bay.

When politicians want to steer citizens in a certain direction in a similar way, we usually talk about "social engineering." In this case, we might call it "media engineering." Two questions that immediately arise are what this media engineering looks like in practice, and what the consequences will be for the image of Sweden.

Our first task is to make a distinction between ethnic identity and citizenship. For a long time, Swedish in the ethnic and civic sense was much the same thing, except for national minorities: the Sami, the Tornedalen Finns, the Roma, and the Jews. With the mix of people we have in Sweden, the distinction between ethnicity and citizenship becomes necessary and a choice situation arises: In the public debate, what should be included in the term "Swedish"?

The choices journalists usually make are demonstrated, for example, by what is written about the journalist Dawit Isaak, who has been imprisoned in Eritrea for more than two decades. He was born in Eritrea, has dark skin and is imprisoned there after having worked as a journalist critical of the Eritrean regime. So why is he called Swedish or, sometimes, Swedish-Eritrean? The answer is simple: he is a Swedish citizen. With that definition, Russian hedge runners, black musicians, dark-skinned footballers and German-born queens can also add their talents to the Swedish nation and contribute to its glory.

Perhaps most importantly, civic nationalism does not draw borders within countries but between them. In the United States, this is the kind of nationalism that under the name of patriotism not only holds together the vast country with all its ethnic groups, but also makes the United States a favourable country for refugees. True or not, the chances of making a decent life for oneself in the U.S seem greater than in Sweden.

Moving on to what is the final paragraph of the "Little Satsjöbad Agreement," the downplaying of criminal activity, there is another important distinction to be made, namely whether or not it is relevant in the context of criminal activity to talk about the perpetrator's ethnicity. It can be difficult to draw the line.

An example: A newspaper reported on a 21-year-old man who was sentenced to a long prison term for three aggravated robberies. In one case he robbed two people at knifepoint of a 1,000 SEK. The next day, he tried to steal cash and a necklace from a 60-year-old woman. A week earlier, he forced a man at knifepoint to withdraw 15,000 SEK from bank ATMs in a town centre and was arrested.

The name of this criminal was easily found on the Internet. The surname was very difficult both to spell and to pronounce. His first name was Abdullah. The question now is which is more informative and relevant: to indicate the town he lives in, his age, or that he is of non-European immigrant stock?

To answer that question, you first need to know something about the kind of crime he committed. Is it a crime that is typical of immigrants, or of certain ethnic groups — or is there no such relevance? To single him out in his role as an immigrant may not be relevant and becomes, if not exactly racism, then opening the door to racist reflections. On the other hand, if this is a crime typical of young men of his kind, then simply calling him a man from the town Västerås is obviously withholding relevant information.

A radical and unethical way of dealing with ethnicity is to give all perpetrators of crimes fictitious Swedish names. This has been tried by *Dagens Nyheter* in a series of articles about young sex offenders under headlines such as "Anders, 15, molested his little brothers" and "Dennis, 15, raped Alexandra in a school toilet."

Readers contacted *Dagens Nyheter* and wondered why they called the 15-year-old Dennis. It could give the impression that the perpetrator was Swedish, which he was not. The reporters defended themselves by saying that Dennis is a name that occurs in many countries. They considered it racist to mark the boys' foreign origin. After discussion in the editorial office, it was eventually decided that the names "should be as close to the real names as possible without pointing them out" — and in the next article, the boys were given the names Jousef and Ahmed.

If journalists choose Swedish names to downplay the criminality of immigrants, one may get the impression that certain types of crime have increased significantly among Swedes. Rape is both a crime that has greatly increased and is clearly over-represented among certain immigrant groups. When it then turns out that it is mostly ethnic Swedish girls who are raped, another choice arises for the journalists. Should they report the truth and thereby, as they see it, promote xenophobia? One leads to the other, and the approach ends up with the media engaging in self-censorship.

Many of those who participate in the public debate(both in the media and online), have grown tired of the hypocrisy resulting from the desire for a multicultural society. Plain language is increasingly important; the reason is that the deeper you dig, the more ideology and political positioning you find in almost everything written about asylum management and immigrants (sometimes quite openly and otherwise almost always between the lines).

## Substandard Leadership

In Western rhetoric, democracy is not only *the best form,* but also *the only acceptable form* of government. The political problem is that the leaders appointed in general elections are not up to the task. Their primary qualification is almost always that they are party loyalists. Their professional careers begin when they, at a young age, join a po- litical youth organisation. These were not originally intended as nurs- eries for professional politicians, but to create politically aware voters. Now they are launching pads for careers which aspire towards the elite strata of politics (in much the same way that Oxford, Cambridge and the London School of Economics are in the UK, the École na- tionale d'administration is in France, and the Ivy League universities are in the US). In Germany, a doctorate is so coveted by top politi- cians that they sometimes cheat their way to one. In Sweden it is not education but party loyalty that is the political currency.

When these ideologically hard-nosed politicians, with the party's wishes as their guiding star, also appoint heads of authorities and other representatives of the state, municipalities and county coun- cils, we get a set of leaders who are not up to the task. In particu- lar, the Social Democrats have exploited the power of appointment. One example is the tenancy rights movement. The journalist Anders Isaksson stated in a 1996 article for the magazine *Modern Times* (Sw. *Moderna Tider*) that rental housing is not compatible with the Social Democratic rhetoric of equality. Why, then, do the Social Democrats want to keep the municipal public housing authorities at almost any cost? The answer is that, in this way, they provide jobs and other benefits for loyal politicians and civil servants.

They are also happy to pass the job on to the next generation. Many ministers' children end up in the political fast lane. But, above all, they trade important and highly paid jobs for loyalty to the party. Let me give you an example:

Anna Johansson is the daughter of the Social Democratic politician who for many years used to be called "Gothenburg's strong man," municipality chairman Göran Johansson. At the age of 17, she dropped out of high school after becoming pregnant. In 1989, she had her first child and three years later her second. In the meantime, she joined the Social Democratic Youth Union (SSU) and started her own SSU club. Her overall education was one year of studies at an adult school.

In 2014, Anna Johansson was handpicked by the Prime Minister Stefan Löfven to be Minister of Infrastructure. She tells us herself: "Stefan was straightforward: 'I want you in my government,' he said. I said, 'have you thought this through?' and of course he had. I promised to give him an answer the next day. Then I called my father. He said 'yes, that's fine, you can do it.'"[1]

Anna Johansson asked Stefan Löfven if he had thought the appointment was reasonable. She didn't even have a driving licence and had never worked on transport and communication issues before. It is unclear what Anna Johansson's qualifications were for the post of minister, both in terms of knowledge of the subject and political competence.

A democratic welfare state such as ours is very fragile, a fact which Swedes in general do not realise. On the contrary, they seem to believe that a democratic welfare state can withstand anything. Because of incompetent politicians, we live in a country that is on the

---

1    https://www.gp.se/nyheter/sverige/anna-johanssons-v%C3%A4g-till-toppen-1.4480929.

skids. At the time of this writing (spring of 2022), widespread riots have rocked several cities. The question that begs an answer is "Why is this happening?"

Two hypotheses: the first, which I have already presented, is that democracy in its Swedish version is unable to produce sufficiently competent leaders. The second is that the democratic process produces leaders who do not put the interests of the people first.

Before the 2018 election, Social Democrat Göran Persson said, "Do not tell me about the Swedish class society. I grew up in it. I hate it." After resigning in year 2006 as Prime Minister, he became a consultant for a PR company and was invited to several company boards, which made it possible for him to buy not only one but two mansions in the county of Sörmland, south of Stockholm. His income in 2009–2020 is estimated at 10 million EUR. The Conservative Prime Minister Fredrik Reinfeldt made a similar career after leaving his post in 2014, with a comparable income. Reports indicate that he charged and received 12,000 EUR for a single lecture in Gothenburg.

I think both hypotheses hold up quite well, but the one with the greatest explanatory power is that politicians no longer represent the people.

According to the EIU's measure of democracy for the year 2021, only 6.4% of the world's population reside in a "full democracy"; this is down slightly from 8.4% in 2020, after two countries (Chile and Spain) were downgraded to "flawed democracies." This year, Sweden ranked number four.[2] No matter which organisation is responsible for compiling this data, Sweden is always in the top five. At the bottom of the list, we find the countries where Swedish politicians recruit "new Swedes," i.e. the Middle East and Africa.

Sweden has the highest per capita asylum and family migration levels in the Western world. Since all human beings are of equal

2   https://www.eiu.com/n/campaigns/democracy-index-2021/?utm_source=teg-website&utm_medium=press_release&utm_campaign=democracy-in-dex-2021.

value, according to current dogma, politicians do not see it as problematic to import young and uneducated Muslim men from the world's most dysfunctional and violent states.

Anyone who does not understand that this poses a very serious threat to the democratic welfare state of Sweden should put on their dunce caps so that those around them understand that this is a person whom we should be nice to, but who absolutely should not be entrusted with any power.

Swedish authorities grant financial aid to people who do not even know where Sweden is. This is where the rhetoric about the equal value of all human beings comes in, as a kind of perverted legitimisation.

Is the extremely generous asylum policy and the international ambitions of Swedish egalitarianism a result of listening to what the people want? Or is the generosity about gaining prestige in the EU and the UN, getting pats on the back from the Bilderbergers and other elite groups in the international community? Even if Swedish politicians will never admit it, the domestic welfare comes fourth in order of importance, following three other priorities:

- party ideology
- media approval
- prestige within the EU (politicians of the EU collective are considered more important)

## An Uninformed Public

A further example of how the best becomes the enemy of the good is that democracy requires an informed electorate. The philosopher who played the greatest political role in the post-war period, Karl Popper, painted the picture of the citizen as a "moral subject," who takes responsibility for the development of society. Otherwise,

democracy does not work. In this, Popper echoed the American sociologist Charles Wright Mills, who argued that democracy presup-
posed an enlightened public.

Enlightened voters are the "good." All citizens getting to
vote—that's "the best." One way to realise the requirement for enlightened voters is to somehow make demands on them. In the early
days of Swedish democracy, the right to vote was linked to the voter's
wealth and income, which was a way of taking responsibility for the
politicians who were entrusted to lead the country. That is not the
case today.

In today's Sweden, as we know, all citizens can vote (including the
mentally disabled and criminal populations). You don't even have to
live in Sweden. If you are an EU citizen, or from Norway or Iceland,
you can vote in municipal and regional elections. This also applies to
immigrants from other countries as long as they have lived in Sweden
for at least three years.

What we have in Sweden are politicians who are not very sup-
portive of their own people's interests. They are brought to power
by voters, who cannot with the best will in the world be seen as an
enlightened public. Neither politicians, who are happy to lay down
foggy words about what democracy is, nor voters, have a clear awareness of what citizens can demand of their elected politicians, or of
what is necessary to create a well-functioning and sustainable society.
In plain language: our politically incompetent leaders come to power
via ignorant citizens.

Well, there was a way to remedy this degenerate form of democracy: *the media*. Television, radio and the press have a fantastic opportunity to fulfil the role they claim (but lie about): not only could
they be the people's agents and steer politicians right, but they could
also provide citizens with the political education that would make
them "an enlightened public." By sitting in the lap of power, by not
doing their job, the gatekeepers of public debate are killing democracy. What they refuse to understand is that they are also pulling

the rug out from under themselves. This is probably one of the main explanations for the breakdown of democratic society. Increasingly, the young generation is abandoning the media for the internet. This is probably one of the main explanations for the breakdown of democratic society.

There are, of course, other ways than the media to create informed voters. This could be a task for the political parties, but here the democratically elected politicians are resisting. They prefer ignorant voters.

This harsh assertion in turn requires an explanation. It is not because politicians are evil or incompetent that they see risks with enlightened voters. It is because politically engaged voters interfere with their job as politicians. Between elections, politicians want to run politics without interference. It is even the case that in the choice between *enlightened* and *misguided* voters, democratic politicians prefer the latter. All political leaders in Sweden lie to citizens in one way or another: sometimes they bluff, sometimes they withhold necessary information, and almost always the valid "truth" is filtered out. The rhetoric of politicians must always be compatible with the ideology of their own political party.

Politicians who are members of a party that is not doing very well never say "Our political ideas are bad, and we'll try to change them so that they lead to a better society. That way we will get more supporters." Instead they say: "We have failed in reaching out with our political programme." In other words, it's about manipulating voters to vote for the "right party." The more disengaged and disinterested voters are, the more likely the political message is to be successful.

To tie in with the theme of this section: that everyone who has reached adulthood should be able to vote, that's "the best." But it has also proven to be "the enemy of good."

## Women Everywhere

Now comes the main focus in this chapter, which addresses feminism and asks a question that many do not want asked: is feminism the enemy of the good society? This is a particularly pressing question, given that Sweden is probably the most feminist nation in the world, both in theory and in practice.

The Dutch social psychologist Geert Hofstede is known for his studies of national values. On two occasions he collected extensive data from IBM employees in 53 countries, first in 1968 and again in 1972. He received 116,000 responses to questions about attitudes and preferences. In the 1970s, he organised the material into five themes and summarised them in a "cultural dimension theory." Hofstede then scored the countries and compared them with each other. His research has attracted a lot of attention, mainly because the conclusions are based on such a large body of material. Hofstede is among the 100 most cited social scientists in the world.

Based on his vast material, Hofstede set no less than 76 criteria for male and female. Japan came first among the masculine countries. Both the United States and Germany are also high on the ranking list. Among the most feminine countries, he placed Sweden in first place, with Norway in second.

This material is now half a century old and Sweden has since been further feminised. At most universities and colleges, women are in the majority among teachers and researchers. In 2021, five out of eight parliamentary parties had female leaders. There were twelve women and eleven men in the government.[3]

In the media, the bias is probably even stronger; I have not looked for studies that show this because it is obvious to me and others who follow Swedish news reporting. Women, women, and more women both report and are interviewed on every conceivable subject. This female expertise covers everything from football and ice hockey

---

3    In the new government 2022 there are 13 male and 11 female ministers.

to advanced and male-dominated high technology, to gang crime, which is almost one hundred percent a male activity. We find out how women think, what they find interesting and how they want to solve various social problems.

One of the most traditionally male professions, law enforcement, is represented in the Police Federation by a woman. In 2019, 33% of Sweden's police officers were women. In total, 44% of all police employees are women. Among civilian employees in the police, women are in the majority, forming a whopping 67%. When 43% of those admitted to the police training programme in Malmö last year were women, Caroline Mellgren, head of the unit for police work and police training at the university, was very happy and hoped that the trend of would continue.

A couple years ago, a young female police officer explained that when she and other female police officers took the metro home from late duty in Rinkeby's new police station, they needed an escort. Rinkeby is an infamous migrant-dominated Stockholm suburb. If there had been only male police officers there, would they have made that demand? Hardly, they would realise it was ridiculous. If they felt unsafe on their own, they would have to arrange to protect each other. But for the female officer, the issue of escort was certainly relevant, and I don't think she would feel entirely comfortable being escorted by another young female officer.

Recruitment films for the Armed Forces are another example. In the American ones, it is crystal clear that the military is a male profession and also a very physically demanding one. In the Swedish ones, either women are the main focus, or the films are gender-neutral.

Now, war is not just any activity: it's about killing enemy soldiers. A country that does not recruit optimally efficient soldiers, but deliberately reduces efficiency for ideological reasons, will be responsible in war for more soldiers dying, both men and women. The reason is that these mixed corps risk having to fight against opponents who are all men. In that case, it is a question of not really wanting to win, which is the same as losing, and since it is a question of war, it can be said to be a form of social suicide. Nor should it be forgotten that in war people are injured. Women are less able than men to cope with injuries.

The Swedish defence does not reason in the above way. For example, Sweden's Nordic Battle Group of elite soldiers had, for many years, a standing lion with a not-very-prominent erect penis in its coat of arms. Outraged by this symbol of masculinity, a group of female soldiers complained to the European Court of Justice. Swedish politicians listened and removed the offensive limb. Swedish heralds protested but were not heard. The lion was literally castrated.

In autumn of 2016, the Swedish Armed Forces released a new handbook for Swedish military personnel. It made it quite clear that in Sweden, the Armed Forces prefer political correctness over efficiency. There are several so-called gender advisors in Swedish units; the goal, according to the authorities responsible for the Swedish Armed Forces, is to be more progressive than other countries. As the book says: "Swedish units can also contribute to raising awareness within multilateral organisations of the importance of the gender perspective. This can be done by developing report formats that include gender and suggesting the integration of the gender perspective at meetings and in plans."

Thus, we have female police officers in Sweden, we have female firefighters, and we have female soldiers. Gender equality is a political goal that is close to the heart of left-liberals.

At the same time, the state reasonably has the responsibility to choose the optimal solution for important public services. I believe that if the people had a choice, the distribution between male and female police officers would be more clearly skewed in favour of the men.

But if the people, for reasons I will not go into here, also choose women for these posts, then it is the duty of the state in a democracy to make not an ideological but *an efficiency-optimal* choice. Which means women in higher positions are welcome, but if physical strength and other male "virtues" are required, then it should be men—and women in particular who meet the requirements placed on men. Ultimately, this is about competence. Police officers in Rinkeby should not have to ask for an external escort when they go home from work.

Is this a reactionary perspective? Yes, insofar as reactionary means reacting, and it is right to react to stupid decisions. I and many others are reacting to the politicisation of society. At its core, it is totalitarian when politicians neither listen to what citizens want, nor look out for the best interests of citizens. In a totalitarian state, ideology wins out over both democracy and optimal choices.

## The Exemplary Citizen

One morning a few years ago, I got the idea to check the number of women and men on the front page of my morning paper. Five pictures showed women. Men were completely absent. The five women included Suzanne Brøgger, a Dane who had written a new novel, and then a female critic for *Dagens Nyheter,* who had also written a new novel. The third picture showed a woman doing strength training and demonstrating that women can maximise their training by considering their menstrual cycle. The fourth picture showed one of the newspaper's own female journalists. The last and largest picture showed a woman in Venezuela sitting, cradling a child in her arms. The picture also showed the back of another woman. It was just another average day for Swedish journalists.

For some time, I have also been monitoring how the state television news programmes *Rapport* and *Aktuellt* choose images and interviewees, and it is noticeable how predominant women are. When choosing between pictures of women and men, Swedish journalists regularly choose women, and this has been the case for several years.

When Sweden and the Western world were subjected to mass immigration in the autumn of 2015, it became almost absurd, as more than 70% of those who streamed across the Swedish border were single young men. This did not stop the media from choosing images of women and families in their reporting, as well as, of course, images of children. As best they could, the young men were screened out.

One lie that the media constantly promotes is that gender discrimination explains why women don't earn as much as men. This is not true. The difference is largely due to the "raw wage gap," which in turn is because women work more part-time and are more likely to be in low-paid jobs. Men invest more in their careers and choose salaries according to performance, while women prefer fixed salaries in secure jobs. It is therefore a matter of life choices. Three very reliable economists showed this in a 2001 study of almost half a million private sector workers: in terms of pay by gender for the same job and the same qualifications, the differences were largely negligible.[4] And why should a good woman be paid less than a good man? Moreover, women now dominate higher education. But the media, which peddles dominant ideologies and especially the elite feminist one, prefers myths and pitting the sexes against each other to that of accurate reporting.

The number of women heads of state agencies is growing. The highest paid director general in 2021 was Lena Erixon, head of the Transport Administration. Today, the number of female and male directors-general is roughly equal, but old inequalities must be atoned for, and responsible politicians have a duty to rein in the patriarchy. In the choice between men and women, women therefore obviously have priority. More women should compensate for an older age with more men.

---

4    Eva M. Meyersson Milgrom, Trond Petersen and Vemund Snartland, "Equal Pay for Equal Work? Evidence from Sweden and a Comparison with Norway and the U.S." *The Scandinavian Journal of Economics* Vol. 103, No. 4 (Dec., 2001).

One of the critical positions taken by advocates of the intellectual "meltdown" of postmodernism is that the injustices of the past can be compensated for in our time — an idea strongly related to Christianity's idea of original sin. Sometimes the children and grandchildren of those murdered in the Nazi death camps claim to be second and third generation victims. Of course, there is no such thing as second and third generation victims. It is about the identification process. The choice is between being a victim and taking full responsibility for one's own life. If we stick to Swedish women, they are not oppressed. They can do as they please, including failing in their most important biological task: bringing children into the world.

Western and Swedish women do not want to have many children because it restricts their freedom. Or, to make the answer more precise and at the same time not quite so controversial: within the feminist elite who control policy on these issues, there is no interest in slowing down female emancipation. Today's elite feminists despise and distance themselves from the traditional role of women. Instead, paradoxically, they model themselves on men and their freedoms. Their aim is to grab as much of the male cake as possible; preferably to take it over.

Feminists compete and fight with men for their power and privileges. They do not readily admit this, but in their rhetoric, they follow two tracks. One is the demand that women must have exactly the same opportunities, pay, etc. as men. The second is the claim that men oppress women. Therefore, men must give up power — sorry — share power with women.

Once women have achieved the goal of *equality*, the struggle will be about *equal outcomes* and ultimately about who should govern society, men or women. It is not that this struggle is ever won. It leads from legitimate demands to pathology. For the victorious women, winning would be tantamount to being thrown back into futility.

## Male Suffrage Questioned

In the *Dalademokraten* newspaper in January 2019, the Social Democratic debater Patrice Soares seriously proposed abolishing male suffrage. The reason he gave was that men are violent and that a couple of years earlier as many as 22,000 cases of sexual assault were reported: 99% of rapes are committed by men, while 98% of rape victims are women.

What he did not mention, however, was which men commit these abuses. P. Jonasson, a private individual who felt that the media was not reporting the truth, took it upon himself to review all convictions for sexual offences in 2012–17. It turned out that men of non-European descent committed 84% of the aggravated rapes. For assault rapes, the figure for convicted foreign men was even higher at 95.6%.[5]

The coming years' parliamentary elections frightened Patrice Soares. He therefore proposed abolishing both male suffrage and male political representation for a trial period of four terms. Until men began to behave civilly again, voting rights and political posts would be restricted to Sweden's women.

The point is, of course, that it is not a woman but a man who is demanding this. He is getting a backlash, though not from any well-known or highly esteemed commentators, but from those in the online community. Even if Soares wrote it with the intention of provoking his audience, there is no getting around the fact that *Dalademokraten* and its editor-in-chief published the article as a serious opinion piece.

Two questions arise. The first is: "how did it come to this"? And the second is whether Sweden can really be a better country if men hand over the political responsibilities to women.

That women are waging a legitimate struggle against the oppressive patriarchy is an image that has been ingrained in Sweden's collective psyche for over a hundred years. Feminism is therefore not

---

5   https://pjjonasson.wordpress.com/.

usually interrogated. It flies under the radar — everyone who enters into public discourse agrees that female emancipation and equality are desirable goals. Women should have the same opportunities, pay, etc. as men.

Since the 1980s, a completely different kind of feminism has developed in this mire, without encountering any major resistance. It is an extreme and sectarian elite feminism, which sees men as its enemy and is more concerned with fighting with them for power than with promoting a greater appreciation of female qualities, and what are traditionally regarded as female tasks. Patriarchy, with its rape culture, is described as a very dangerous enemy. It is therefore unsurprising that these elite feminists are working for the disintegration of the nuclear family; for them, a divorced woman is a happy woman and a single woman with children lives a better life than if she lived with a man.

According to feminists, not only women but also homosexuals, transgender people, immigrants, and ethnic minorities are victims of patriarchy. They are subject to the greatest oppression and injustice. Their interests must therefore be given priority. The argument is that the primary task of politics is to ensure the equal value of all.

Sectarian feminism might not be so much to talk about — there are several sects in our country — if it hadn't taken hold at the very top of the power hierarchy. The propagandistic image of men as potential rapists, wife beaters, and objects of derision is spread at all levels, including by state organisations. Most of it is untrue, but this is how feminists manage to show that they are making an urgent political contribution to a fully egalitarian Sweden.

Feminism is a fundamental cornerstone of both left and right-wing political logic. In this sense, feminism in Sweden is perhaps the most important tool at the disposal of the political class. They claim that men's time is over. That frightens me — not because I am a man, but because I think I know what this means is happening to society.

## Society Building

It is men who build societies. Whether evil men addicted to power, or good democratic men, it's always men! This is true not only of totalitarian societies, but also of democracies and welfare societies. Women have their role, and it should not be belittled or denied. But it is no accident that the female mind is not at the helm.

Genetically, it is an absurd idea that men and women should fight each other for power; to carry on humanity, the sexes must work together. There are no (other) mammals where the sexes compete for power. Although there are tensions and grey areas, both males and females know what their main tasks are. These primary gender roles run into each other's territories and can, to some extent, swap places with each other. But the flexibility is not limitless.

Both skills are necessary, but community building comes first. If there is no functioning society with laws, security, consistency among decision-makers and rules of the game based on experience, it will not be possible to arrange a good life there, no matter how empathetic the governing politicians and opinion-formers are.

Neither anthropologists, historians, nor political scientists know of any functioning matriarchies, i.e. societies where women are in power. This does not mean that it is wrong for a woman to sit at the top of the pyramid of power. It is not that women are not good enough, but that the female mind does not work for governing society. Matriarchy, especially a functioning modern matriarchy, is nothing more than a fantasy.

The society that men build is uninhabitable until women have done their share of the work. It is woman who creates "liveability" and breathes life into society with her existence and that of her children. Men's dependence on women does not stop there. If, for whatever reason, women do not bear enough children, the family, the tribe and their own people die out. Men may oversee women, but women oversee life and death, even existence itself—and thus also men.

## Feminist Government Policy

Upon taking office in 2014, the Social Democratic government claimed to be the first feminist government in the world. This was also true of Sweden's foreign policy, which Foreign Minister Margot Wallström declared to be feminist.[6] On its website, the social democratic government presented the world's first feminist government and there the term gender equality appeared five times! So, what does gender equality mean to the government? The answer is given on the same home page:

> Gender equality is about equality between women and men, who should have the same opportunity to shape society and their own lives. This includes issues such as power, influence, economy, education, work and physical integrity.[7]

If you then read how the ministers are presented, it becomes almost parodically clear that gender equality and general equality are key concepts for the Social Democratic government that has just resigned. It's all about equality, the concept that governs how Swedish politicians think and how the world should be described.

Do the Swedish people really want to invest in gender equality first and foremost? Is equal treatment of LGBTQ+ people a pressing political issue?[8] Does it reflect the will of the people that those who

---

6    After the 2022 election, Sweden has a bourgeois government and one of its first decisions was to scrap the feminist foreign policy. However, it will probably return if the left wins the election in four years.

7    https://www.regeringen.se/artiklar/2021/03/regeringens-arbete-for-jamstalld-het-ar-viktigare-an-nagonsin/.

8    The acronym LGBTQI originated in the US in the 1990s and is made up of the first letters of the words "lesbian," "gay," "bisexual," "transgender," "queer" and "intersex." The latter two terms were added in the 2000s, and are now

are in the country illegally should also get a share of the tax-funded welfare? Is it self-evident that entry-level labour market wages should be equal for all, when it is known that this not only closes the labour market to many immigrants but also feeds the low-wage black market?

Sweden is governed by an elite that has not bothered to ask the people what is and what is not important to them. It goes without saying that equality is an overriding ideal. Swedish men in decision-making positions do not fight back, but share the view that male privilege must be limited. However, it is possible that there is a certain tenacity or silent resistance among the men in power.

Equality presupposes a Marxist-feminist interpretation of the world with oppressors and oppressed. The division of roles is a given: white men are evil, while white women are oppressed. Dark-skinned women are doubly oppressed, etc. The task of the "good guys" is to save the oppressed. It is this division of roles that determines which story will be told. Reality is subordinated to these ideological claims.

The government would like to see equality in the business world as well. In the spring of 2016, many Swedish newspapers reported that the proportion of women on the boards of listed companies was slowly but surely increasing. But the government felt it was going too slowly and threatened to introduce a quota law to reach the 40% target.[9]

However, it has not proved so easy for politicians to govern business life with directives. In the autumn of the same year, Minister of Economic Affairs Mikael Damberg reintroduced a proposal to fine listed companies with less than 40% female board members. In January 2017, it was withdrawn because it failed to gain support in Parliament. In 2021, the percentage of female board members was

----

sometimes joined by "A" for "asexual" and a plus sign or asterisk as a placeholder for other identities.

9    https://www.di.se/artiklar/2016/4/14/missar-kvoteringsmalet/.

still 38%. This placed Sweden among the EU countries with the highest proportion of women on the boards of listed companies.

What happens to a society where feminism is the tool that the power elite uses to create an egalitarian society? I would like to highlight three effects:

- A society is governed by laws, rules and norms. Women tend to see personal relationships as more important than following the rules, because that is what is done in well-functioning families. For society, this is destructive. The consequence is the breakdown of norms.

- A society must be able to both maintain and enforce its monopoly on violence. Women dislike violence as a problem-solving method, which leads to a weakening of the state's monopoly on violence.

- The state has negative and positive sanctions at its disposal to control citizens. Men tend to resort to negative sanctions, i.e. punishing those who do wrong, while women prefer to opt for positive sanctions, i.e. rewarding those who do right. A feminist society thus opens the door to those forms of crime where only negative sanctions help.

The government's declaration of the fundamental importance of equality seems strange, given the gigantic difficulties that Sweden faces. The crisis has, since the Second World War, never been as great as it is now. And just what are the politicians in the Parliament doing? Well, they are happy to pounce on issues such as a third free month for fathers, which is defined as an important gender equality issue. The politicians become the parents of the people, while we voters are the children, the ones who must be educated but never really become adults.

## Female Cruelty

Like members of other political sects, many elite feminists engage in infighting. Ostracism campaigns, toxic Twitter wars, and the so-called "trashing" of opponents are common. On Facebook, there are groups with hundreds of members, mostly devoted to writing down female opinion leaders who are distasteful to them. As one feminist noted, "Sisterhood is powerful, it can kill sisters."

The militant branch of Swedish feminism is crueller than perhaps any other ideological movement in Sweden. I am not alone in this view. Among my notes, I find the following quote. Unfortunately, I don't know who wrote it, nor when. I can't even tell if it's a man or a woman who wrote it down, but I suspect it's a woman. I'd like to think that a man doesn't really have the right to be so off his toes — there's a good chance he'll just be dismissed as a misogynist:

> Swedish feminism is the sickest thing I've encountered in my entire lifetime. Since when did it become an important women's issue to hate men, bully teenage boys, and agitate in the thousands against anyone who disagrees with their worldview? Yes, I actually think that feminism today is more like an autoimmune disease, attacking its own system, humanity at its foundations. As a kind of collective mass psychosis. Self-hatred that has nothing whatsoever to do with women's issues. Keep me safe! Get as far away from me and my children as you possibly can. Now! Don't ever come near me. Just stay as far away as possible.

When I Googled the text, I ended up at a Facebook link from 5 April 2020 celebrating the 15th anniversary of Sweden's first feminist party: "Congratulations to us all!" This party, Feminist Initiative (FI), never managed to get beyond the extreme sect stage, but as we know, feminism won. I wonder a bit about the charismatic Gudrun Schyman, the founder of the party. Her sins are well-attested:

**1996:** Premiere of the film *Secrets and Lies* at Sveavägen in Stockholm. During the performance, Gudrun Schyman needs to pee, but cannot be bothered to go to the toilet, so she sits down in the aisle to do her business. Her wet panties are thrown to the audience.

**1997:** Swedish television's news program *Rapport* records Gudrun Schyman confessing to drunk driving. The chief medical officer of the Swedish Road Administration says that her driving licence should be withdrawn, as the chief medical officer considers her to be an alcoholic.

**1998:** Gudrun Schyman hires her own daughter and her 16-year-old friend as cleaning help off the books.

**1999:** Gudrun Schyman has problems accounting for purchases of more than 250,000 SEK on the credit card belonging to the Parliament. The expenses relate to taxis, hotels, and air travel. Receipts are completely missing.

**2002:** Gudrun Schyman likens Swedish men to the Afghan Taliban.

**2003:** Gudrun Schyman moves from Stockholm to a town in southern Sweden and at the same time makes a financial move. Tax-free rent subsidies and allowances increase her income by more than 100,000 SEK a year.

**2003:** It is discovered that Gudrun Schyman will lose her post as leader of the Left Party. She then tries to make tax deductions for travel and restaurant visits that the party or Parliament have already paid for.

**2003:** Gudrun Schyman accepts a 50-day fine, which means she admits to tax offences. The prosecutor says that "a fifty-day fine indicates that it is a qualified fine offence."

**2010:** Gudrun Schyman burns up 100,000 SEK in Almedalen, the annual event of the Swedish political class, to get attention.

Now that's a CV worthy of a professional politician who wants to lead a feminist political party! Schyman started the party in 2005, after a period in Parliament, as a political wild card. At one of the party's

first meetings, the participants sang the fight song "Fucking old man"
(Sw. *Jävla gubbe*) Here are the first seven lines:

OLD MAN FUCKING MAN
DESTROYING OUR WORLD WITHOUT SHAME
RAPES, WARS, FIGHTS AND DESTROYS
UNDERSTAND THAT YOU CAN'T OR SHOULDN'T
TAKE ME IN THE PUSSY WHEN YOU GET HORNY
OR ON MY BREASTS WHEN YOUR DESIRE FALLS ON
I HATE YOU, YOU FUCKING MAN

And the last three lines:

BECAUSE HERE YOU SEE A WOMAN
WHO HATES YOU SO MUCH
WE'LL TEAR YOU TO PIECES

This unpleasant text makes me remember something that the Nobel
Prize winner Doris Lessing said a few decades ago: "We live in an age
when stupid, uneducated, and mean women can vilify the kindest,
gentlest and most intelligent men, without anyone protesting." Then
I react to the more than legitimately lame rhymes and think that I
could do something about them, but I realize that I'm one of those
"fucking old men," so the feminists probably wouldn't be interested in
my help. Well, anyway, it was good that FI made it clear what miserable creatures Swedish men are.

It should be added that men and women often show aggression in
different ways. Men tend to defend themselves with physical attacks
while women, naturally enough, defend themselves with elaborate
verbal attacks. Women therefore have an advantage, as men very
rarely attack women physically. Female aggression can be unbeliev-
ably vicious and take the form of reputation destruction.

Directly at one of Canadian psychology professor Jordan
Peterson's visits to Sweden, this aggression type also got a face
through our own Foreign Minister Margot Wallström, who asked

Jordan Peterson to crawl back under his rock (vicious) and then added that he was completely uninteresting (reputation destruction). The same behaviour was also displayed in other contexts towards the leaders of various countries. Even Centre Party leader Annie Lööf asks men to "crawl back under their rocks" on Twitter.

I am testing the hypothesis that this nastiness is really about alienation. In Islam, men have rock-hard control over women. There is no question of gender equality or female emancipation. That should result in a rich literature in which secular Muslim women attack men and their oppression. However, the feminist nastiness and lamentations are almost completely absent. This raises the question why Swedish and Western women, so successful in the battle between the sexes, are so aggressive and dissatisfied. Is it an inverted dissatisfaction with the new role of women? Under today's Swedish paradigm of opinion, women are not allowed to be women and men not to be men. I suspect that our basic identities, acquired through evolution, are denied.

## The Nice Women

Women think that if we are nice to other people, they will be nice back. Everyone should join in, no one should be left out! There is a curious contradiction between how vicious and hateful feminists can be towards other women and their own men and how generous and forgiving they can be towards those whom they see as harmed by society — the "unfortunate children." When police and social services in 2017 failed to deal with Moroccan criminals, so-called "street children," who essentially made their living by stealing and mugging, *Dagens Nyheter*'s editorial writer Lisa Magnusson wrote that

> children are worth protecting precisely because they are small and fragile. And we have an obligation to care for and protect street children too, even if they are both unreliable and untrustworthy, even if their future is never so bleak. To be their mothers and fathers when they have none, and close

the door on the dangerous underworld — literally. That's looking out for their best interests.[10]

Nobody cared about those who were robbed and raped by these criminal youngsters. It was the children who were pitied; those who had to live on the streets.

The model describing human existence in terms of oppressor and oppressed is fundamentally female. The oppressed suffer, and the female mind has empathy as perhaps its most important foundation. Those who suffer must be helped! The definition of a good society is that it is on the side of the oppressed.

The wave of mass immigration which occurred in the autumn of 2015, with its predominance of aggressive and uncivilised men, did not set off the alarm among Swedish women. On the contrary, they were received as vulnerable people whom Swedes could take care of and help. Feminised Sweden met them at the border stations with welcome signs. Let the young men without passports or other identifying documents come into the country, let them stay and go to the same school as all the other children! The fact that they have no identity documents is absolutely appalling. Everyone must now be especially kind to those who are having such a hard time.

Thinking, to deserve to be called thinking, must hold emotions in check. Acting in accordance with what one feels is not the same as restraining one's emotions and thus "purifying" thinking. However, there is no absolute dividing line between thinking and feeling. All thinking is filtered through our emotions. There is a clear difference between male and female here. The female "filter" is much denser and more easily activated than the male filter, i.e. women's feelings about how problems should be solved are much stronger than men's.

Female thinking is also more socially oriented than male thinking, which is related to one of the main tasks of women: raising

10  https://www.dn.se/ledare/signerat/lisa-magnusson-vi-maste-gora-nagot-at-gatubarnen.

children. Incidentally, this difference is also captured in the template of how men and women view potential partners. Men are attracted to women as they are, hoping they will not change (age, becoming bitches, etc.), while women see men more as projects to be shaped into what they want them to be.

Women don't want to see the guns of the state. They are not prepared to defend their country, because they dislike violence. At a time of recurring terrorist crimes, they form hearts of hands, light candles and say we must forgive. With a feminist view of society, it is even possible to integrate the invasive Muslims, those who abhor multiculturalism — just give them a big hug! They refuse to see that Muslims do not want to integrate at all.

Sweden got the world's first feminist government, but along with it came a broken defence force and a weakened state monopoly on violence. Men who think like men understand the gravity of the situation. What the young suburban men (immigrants) are doing when they burn police cars and stop emergency vehicles is asserting their territory and defending their residential area against the "intruders," i.e., the blue-light officials, that is the police and emergency services. They say that this society is theirs and "you can take your dreams of integration and community somewhere where the sun never shines." Dialogue cops want to grill sausages and talk to violent criminals, but don't dare enter an ever-growing number of "outlying" areas. In Australia, throwing stones at community blue-light officials can lead to up to 14 years in prison. Not in Sweden.

Western civilisation is militarily unbeatable. It is the strongest there has ever been. But women are its weak point. Feminism is one of the forces destroying Western civilisation. More precisely, it is the link between female power and state power that is dangerous. When women take over, men are not allowed to use the necessary violence.

The damage is probably irreparable. The only solution is a return to a society where men regain control over women, and that is unlikely to happen. Western men, even in their most private dreams, do not want to dominate women in that way.

## What Women Are Attracted To

The fact that women decide who can have sex and who can repro-duce has very far-reaching consequences. Deep down, men know that if they lose this power, if women themselves gain control over their sexuality, women will be overpowering them. Men are prepared to do almost anything to get sex. The Western man would even rather give up his manhood than risk losing the favour of women.

That's how Swedish men become nice wimps, *"svennar,"* not real men. Male qualities such as courage, honour, self-confidence and self-discipline are lost. Our leaders can't defend our Western culture because they don't know how to behave as men. They have lost their masculinity. They do not dare to fight back.

Swedish boys are cowards, as many immigrant boys learn at school. Men from Africa and the Middle East countries only respect strong men, not strong women. They see women as weak. Men who behave like women are also weak. Then you can do what you want.

As the quick-witted actress Mae West once put it: "When women get stray, men follow in their tracks."

Women have their biological radar set on men who can protect them and their children. Aggression and masculine charisma are qualities that attract women. For nice guys who go out of their way to please women, it can be hard to digest that women so often fall for men who will make them miserable.

The fact that women do not think the same way as men when choosing a partner is shown, for example, by what a seventeen-year-old girl wrote in Expressen, after a major highway robbery:

> Another reason for stealing cars and robbing old ladies is to get what you want. I'm not referring to things you can buy in stores. I'm talking about getting the most attractive girls and getting respect from the most

influential guys. I don't know how it is in the rest of Sweden, but where I live I know that there are few girls who are really looking for the Big Love. Another word that explains them is: Golddiggers. Who would say no to the guy in the new Porsche? Who would say no to the guy in the new villa? Who would say no to a date in the most expensive restaurant? Well, when you're a student, almost completely broke and unemployed, not many people would say no. Especially if the guy in question is "famous" in the area.

A guy friend of mine had been in love with a girl for almost three years. He was classed as the school nerd and no one even looked his way. You know how the story ends. He chose the criminal path, got filthy rich and could choose anyone he wanted. Including the chick he'd been chasing for so many years. Pathetic, isn't it?[11]

I am not suggesting that this is a common and "normal" way for young women to choose partners but am limiting myself to the observation that among women, there is a biologically based attraction to strong men, and that strength can be interpreted in many ways. This does not prevent most people from realising that the best choice is the good-looking young man who is investing in his accountancy studies. But then it is reason and not biology that rules. Like men, women are biologically shaped to live in a bygone society, more brutal and more primitive.

Another example of how women think differently from men is that men in prison often receive love and admiration mail from women they do not know:

Anders Eklund, who murdered ten-year-old Engla in Stjärnsund and Pernilla Hellgren in Falun, was contacted by a mother of two who began visiting him in prison after he was convicted of the murders and placed in prison. Christer Karlsson, President of the Association for the Revenge of Criminals in Society, experienced first-hand the attraction of convicted criminals. He was placed in the forensic psychiatric clinic in Huddinge for an investigation after being convicted of drug and violent crimes. He

---

11   https://www.expressen.se/debatt/ranarna-gor-oss-stolta-och-trygga/.

placed a personal ad with the headline "Prisoner looking for…" He immediately received 50 responses.[12]

Women's power is further enhanced by the fact that they are more social and group/consensus oriented than men. Once they begin to gain positions of power, they are backed by their peers. Moreover, as they advance to important positions in politics and to managers in the media, they can influence the flow of information in society. This becomes a self-reinforcing process which, when it has gone as far as it has in Sweden, is almost impossible to stop. In today's Sweden, women control a large part of both formal and informal power.

The men become insecure. Less than ever, they understand women. In feminist Sweden, the good men don't really know how to act. But they do know that women are dangerous, that they can turn on them, whether it's Gudrun Schyman's heiress on the prowl, or some #MeToo trend sweeping through society.

This does not mean that women "win." They also lose. Encroaching on men's territory does not make women happy. It is not power but community and harmonious interaction that makes both women and men happy. Where there is a struggle for power, there is little room for love. We live in a time when the interplay between the sexes is out of kilter. Aristotle's and Darwin's idea that human ethics must be based on human nature no longer applies.

## Women's Left Turn

The sexual revolution of the 1960s ushered in the fall of Western civilisation. The link between sex and marriage was broken. The pill played a major role in this emancipation. Young women no longer had to forego the pleasures of sex because of the risk of pregnancy. One of the consequences was a small group of men being very

12  https://www.expressen.se/nyheter/inloggad/darfor-lockas-kvinnor-av-de-farliga-mannen/.

attractive to many women, which in turn meant that a lot of men were once again rejected, as was the case before industrialism. They were lucky if they met someone who wanted to be with them at all. Winner takes all.

But the winner also surrenders. There are always more women to conquer; the one on the other side of the fence is probably younger and prettier. The risk increases that women, despite the pill, will still be single mothers. Economically, of course, this is problematic for the state, which is faced with an accelerating expense that used to land on the man and the nuclear family. Single mothers cost the Swedish state more than 2 billion SEK a year.

Politically, there is also a change. Biologically, women are traditional. Change brings risks, which threaten their security and thus their existence and that of their children. This was particularly evident in the early trade union movement, where men striking for better conditions had not only employers to contend with but also their women. With the sexual liberation, the rules of the game changed and women swung politically to the left. Welfare becomes even more important to them as a guarantee that they can support themselves and their children if the man gallops on to greener pastures.

When welfare and emancipation are combined, the necessity of the nuclear family diminishes. This is very serious, because the successful Western state has the nuclear family as its main building block.

Swedes are a people who put a lot of energy into being at the cutting edge. If engineers are to be created, then we will ensure that the best are created in Sweden. Should women be liberated? Yes, indeed! Are feminists to run the country? Better there too.

We will have a society where the women of the public are aggressive and see it as their task to overthrow patriarchy. A male regulatory framework is to be forcibly exchanged for a female one. Women become "more masculine." Men shape themselves according to this new ideal and become "more feminine." Men become dissatisfied with these aggressive and demanding women. Women become dis-satisfied with these wimps of men. My hypothesis is that both sexes really want the previous power relationship back, the kind of com-plementary couple relationship that they are genetically instructed to value. It's not just about the "other" in the relationship. Women thrive on being female, men on being male, not the other way around.

# Statist Individualism

## State Abuses

FAMILIES AND clans are strong and potentially dangerous opponents for a nation's elite, while individuals are weak and open to indoctrination. Individualism thus becomes a tool for the elite, which prefers loyal, obedient and harmless citizens, susceptible to manipulation. Clans and other collectives can resist and turn their backs to government power; individuals are less able to do so. Sweden, with a people that is usually described as the most individualised in the world, becomes the perfect place for politicians who wish to test new ideas. Here, it is possible for the elite to destroy their own society, even to replace their own people, almost without resistance.

Swedes are politically weak, not to say "ethnically banned" in their own homeland, while Roma, Jews, Syrians and Kurds, to name a few strong groups, are affirmed. For their members, the collective is a kind of insurance against ruin, the role that the welfare state has taken over for all citizens, i.e. also for ethnic groups that are capable of managing on their own.

To implement individualism without encountering resistance, individualism is conceptualised as something solely positive. The elite say that individualism is freedom, not weakness. Swedes' individualism should be interpreted as citizens living autonomously and thinking independently. Great! Who wouldn't want to be an individualist with that limited description?

The road to individualism, the "liberation," is a long process in which Sweden's land divisions in the 19th century play a major role. The aim, of course, was not to break up village communities and individualise the peasants with their families and households, but it undoubtedly had that effect. Thus, the foundations were laid and, unlike most countries in the rest of Europe at that time, local communities were significantly weakened in Sweden.

Sjöbo, a municipality in southern Sweden, probably showed the last strong local resistance in Sweden. In 1988, Sjöbo had a referendum and said no to accepting 15 refugees. The leader of the Centre political party, Sven-Olle Olsson, declared: "All of us who live in Sjöbo have to understand that Lebanese who come from a culture of violence do not stop being criminals overnight."

Sjöbo became totally degraded and "the spirit of Sjöbo" became a shameful concept. In public, no one thought it was reasonable that the inhabitants of a small community like Sjöbo should have any influence on who would live there. The fact that the Sjöbo people risked having to contribute to their livelihood was not even seen as a valid reason for opposition.

Before the 2018 elections, there were only a few wealthy municipalities where the residents were able to resist when the state, via the Swedish Migration Agency, wanted them to accept an influx of "new Swedes," as well as refugee settlements. The high-status municipalities of Danderyd and Täby north of Stockholm did not allow themselves to be ignored in any way, nor did the bourgeois Östermalm in central Stockholm. This did not mean that the inhabitants took controversy, as Sjöbo did, but they did their best to slip away, without attracting media attention.

At the present time, there are also two municipalities in southern Sweden where the national and conservative political party, the Sweden Democrats, are in power: Hörby and Sölvesborg.[1] The left-

---

1    In Sölvesborg, the Sweden Democrats won the municipal election in 2022 as well, but when the conservatives surprisingly merged with the Social

liberal media are merciless towards them. In Sölvesborg, the Pride flag is not being raised, and the municipality is doing its best to get rid of the Roma beggars.

## Everyone Is an Individual

The concept of *statist individualism* was coined by Swedish historians Henrik Berggren and Lars Trägårdh in 2009.[2] It is now established in the Swedish debate. Wikipedia provides an excellent definition:

> Statist individualism is an ideology which pushes for an alliance between state and individual. The ideology's basic tenet is the idea that a strong state and individual freedom are not mutually exclusive, but that state interference can strengthen personal autonomy.[3]

Berggren and Trägårdh link the concept to modern Sweden, but somewhat contradictorily they also write that Swedish statist individualism has been cultivated for at least a couple of hundred years, after which they cite a long list of famous names from Swedish history.

Taking successful Swedes with well-developed egos in order to prove that Swedes like statist individualism is, methodically speaking, perhaps not the best of approaches. Nevertheless, I think the authors are right. While reading their book, I came up with a few examples of my own that reinforced their perspective. The first was a TV report about how Germans were responsible for their parents when they became old and decrepit and needed extended services and care. Then the children had to contribute financially, if they had that opportunity. It was taken for granted in Germany. In Sweden it is not so. The municipality steps in and takes full financial responsibility. They don't even bother to check whether the immediate family or other

---

Democrats, they lost the rule over the municipality.

2   Henrik Berggren & Lars Trägårdh, *Är svensken människa? Gemenskap och oberoende i det moderna Sverige* (Norstedts, 2015).

3   https://sv.wikipedia.org/wiki/Statsindividualism.

relatives can take responsibility, but instead treats us all as independent individuals.

Another example is when a private school in the northern city of Umeå allowed a seven-year-old Muslim girl to make an important decision. Either she had to take off her veil at school or choose another school. Both the National Agency for Education (Skolverket) and the Discrimination Ombudsman (DO) took the school management to task. After all, this was about the individual's right to choose and have their religious symbols recognised. What the National Agency for Education and the Discrimination Ombudsman (DO) do not seem to have discussed was that the seven-year-old girl did not make this choice individually. It was probably her parents who made the choice. In a sense, it was also her religion that made the choice. The veil is a very complex issue, but in the eyes of the Swedish state, it appeared to be simply an issue of individual freedom.

A third example is the police uniform and the right to wear a turban, kippah or headscarf. Anyone who so wishes has the right to wear one with the uniform. In other words, the state allows individual religious identity to encroach on the symbolic space of collective professional identity.

## Tribalisation

Democracy is based on citizens voting according to their socio-economic positions, but with the "common good" in mind. If Sweden were totally dominated by ethnic Swedes, this perspective would be self-evident, but the question is whether it applies to multicultural Sweden, which is made up of ethnic, cultural, and religious groups that put their own communities first. The "good of one's own group" takes precedence over "the common good," as is the case even in feminism and the LGBTQ movement. It is also particularly true for Muslims who have grown up in clan-controlled countries.

This means that the party or parties that promote Muslim interests, for example, can capture clan voting and collective voting, which upsets the democratic rules of the game. Politics will then no longer be about building the good society, a shared national responsibility, but about optimising the conditions for one's own group. Such tribalisation is another death blow to the democratically governed nation and a consequence of the multicultural ideology.

## Conformists

*The Word Values Survey* map often cited in debates shows that Sweden is a country of extreme individualism.[4] Since individualism and collectivism are opposing concepts, this should mean that Sweden is a country with a cacophony of voices, a country where it is difficult to discern patterns in what people think about things, because most people seem to function according to their own heads, rather than joining the Swedish collective. But that's not the case at all. On the contrary, Swedes, especially those who have access to the public sphere, are extremely similar in their opinions and behaviour. In the second part of his autobiographical *My Struggle* the Norwegian author Karl-Ove Knausgård, then living in Sweden, wrote:

> Exactly how compliant the country is, is beyond description. Also because conformity shows up as an absence; there are actually no other opinions in the public sphere than the prevailing ones. It takes time to discover such things.[5]

In Sweden, beneath the democratic surface, it is the state that decides and sets the standards for how citizens should live their lives. This applies to child rearing, compulsory preschool with gender education, punitive taxes on fuel, what cultural heritage should include, immigration, multiculturalism, costly symbolic policies for the climate,

---

4   https://www.iffs.se/world-values-survey/.

5   Karl Ove Knausgaard, *My Struggle*. Book 2 (Farrar, Straus and Giroux, 2014).

politicised research and government, electricity production without nuclear power, freedom of expression, etc. The list is almost endless. A majority of parliamentary parties broadly agree that it is the job of politicians to regulate citizens' lives in detail. The price of strong statist individualism is a weak civil society.

Even for high status persons in Sweden, it is not possible to fight with the political elite without losing their reputation and social position. See, for example Carl Gustaf XVI, the king and head of state the nation of Sweden. The pride he is expected to have in being Swedish comes with the office. But a king who even hints that the most nationalist party, the Sweden Democrats, is doing anything of value? Forget it!

Perhaps statist individualism explains why Swedes, unlike the French, for example, have such confidence in the state? All Swedes are "children of the state" and people prefer not to criticise their parents. After all, it is they who provide the security in life. Swedes are not used to taking the initiative themselves in matters that are defined as political.

# Liberal Democracy

## EU Liberalism

I AM NOT alone in taking an interest in Hungary, a country which, with a strong leader supported by the majority of the people, has managed to resist the globalisation and social disintegration spreading in the West. After 12 years in power, Viktor Orbán and the national conservative *Fidesz* won another crushing victory in April 2022, receiving 53% of the vote — an even bigger victory than four years earlier.

Most pundits thought the election would be very close and hoped Orbán would be voted out, but it was not to be. The united opposition, a coalition of six parties from the left to the far right, obtained only 35%. The main reason, presumably, was that they had no programme apart from hatred of Orbán that united them.

Viktor Orbán's victory in an election organised according to the rule book did not prevent the leading Swedish morning paper *Dagens Nyheter* from, less than a week later, calling Orbán an autocrat — a synonym for dictator, tyrant and despot:

> Since Orbán's Fidesz took power for the second time in 2010, liberal democracy in Hungary has been effectively dismantled. The courts are now under the control of the government. Around 80% of national news media

are controlled directly or indirectly by Fidesz, according to a review by the European Federation of Journalists.[1]

How is it possible to call a political leader who has just won a general election an autocrat? In my opinion, Hungary is the EU's most democratic country, and Orbán a more democratic leader than any other of the EU's politicians and high bureaucrats. Is the liberal democracy that *Dagens Nyheter* writes about something else than democracy? The British journalist William Nattrass comments in the English magazine *The Spectator*:

> Hungarians — like most central Europeans — don't want to be saved by their politicians. Twentieth-century communism left people in this region deeply suspicious of utopian political ideals. Most don't want a socialist utopia, or a utopia of 'European values': they want pragmatism, positivity, and respect for tradition. Fidesz offers these by the bucketload. The United Opposition offered confusion, negativity, and a desire to sacrifice traditional social policies on the altar of the EU liberalism that Orban defines himself against. As long as it continues to do so, Orbán will keep winning.[2]

It is no coincidence that *The Spectator* writes about EU-liberalism. Several researchers, including German sociologist Wolfgaang Streeck of the Max Planck Institute, see the European Union as an empire with liberal democracy as the unifying ideology. He also sees it as an empire on the verge of collapse.[3] Orbán himself said he has made the following observations during the eleven years he has made numerous and recurring trips to Brussels:

> The European elites, the political decision-makers and those who control the media, imagine that the liquidation of our national identities is a step forward for humanity; that it is not modern to be Polish, Czech or Hungarian, that it is not modern to be Christian. Instead, a new identity has taken their place, the European identity... The British have said no,

1 https://www.dn.se/ledare/klam-at-autokraten-orban-dar-det-verkligen-kanns/.

2 https://www.spectator.co.uk/article/why-viktor-orb-n-keeps-winning.

3 https://www.spectator.co.uk/article/why-viktor-orb-n-keeps-winning.

they want to remain British... The European identity does not exist. There are Poles, there are Hungarians. All the signs in Europe suggest that a cultural counter-revolution is possible.[4]

This comment can be complemented by the one made by former Polish Foreign Minister Witold Waszczykowski in 2016. Then he said that the government's task was "to cure our state of certain diseases" spread by hostile media organs, convinced that the direction of history necessarily leads to "a mixture of cultures and races, a world of cyclists and vegetarians who rely solely on renewable energy and fight all religious symbols." He added that these pathologies were incompatible with the values shared by the majority of Poles who look to "tradition, historical consciousness, patriotism, belief in God, a normal family life between a man and a woman."[5]

## Protecting Your Nation

Why is Viktor Orbán being blamed for turning Hungary into a one-party state? Firstly, because he wants to revise the constitution so that it says "No foreign population can be placed in Hungary." The background is that the EU wants to force Hungary to accept immigrants and that the EU should decide the number. The Hungarian government also wants it to be stated that "the defence of our constitutional identity, which is rooted in our historical constitution, is the fundamental responsibility of the state" and that it is "the responsibility of every state institution to defend Hungary's constitutional identity."

It is hard to understand the criticism. That an openly nationalist party wants to defend the nation against immigration has nothing to do with totalitarianism.

4   https://blogs.lse.ac.uk/brexit/2019/03/06/long-read-the-european-union-is-a-liberal-empire-and-it-is-about-to-fall/.

5   Olivier Bault, "Orbán et Kaczynski pour une contre-révolution culturelle en Europe," *Présent* (9 September 2016) https://present.fr/2016/09/09/Orbán-et-kaczynski-pour-une-contre-revolution-culturelle-en-europe.

In autumn 2016, the country's largest daily newspaper, the opposition left-wing *Népszabadság*, was closed on the grounds that it was financially failing. Critics and journalists claimed it was just a matter of silencing opposition voices.

Four MPs of the social liberal opposition Democratic Coalition decided to boycott the Hungarian Parliament for an indefinite period. In other words, they behaved in the same way as other liberals around Europe: they are unable to see their ideologies challenged and are not prepared to defend them even in a parliamentary debate.

I am not very knowledgeable about Hungary, but what I see is a political party and a political leader taking up the fight with the totalitarian forces that, in the name of democracy, are attacking the nation — that is, the only geopolitical entity compatible with democracy in the true sense of the word.

Perhaps Hungary is becoming one of Europe's last democracies: a country where the political leadership respects the will of the people and defends both its people and its country with the necessary firmness.

## The Wrong Kind of Democracy

What is *democracy*? Simple, it's government by the people. People vote on issues and the alliance or alliances that manage to gather the most votes win. A four-point scale can be set up, based on which model has the greatest capacity to represent the "will of the people":

1)  Best: Direct elections and decisive referendums

2)  Very good: Representative elections and decisive referendums

3)  Pretty good: Representative elections and consultative referendums

4)  Good, but minimum: representative elections

After the Second World War, it became clear that the enemies of democracy can use democracy to destroy it. That is why the West German constitution was given constitutional protection in 1949: It is not permitted to misuse civil rights such as freedom of speech and of the press, freedom of assembly and organisation, secrecy of correspondence and others, in order to combat the free democratic basic order. The highly respected political scientist Samuel P. Huntington therefore made an important distinction when he noted that governments that come to power through universal suffrage may be inefficient, corrupt, short-sighted, unaccountable, dominated by special interests and unable to adopt policies that are demanded by the public, but this does not make them undemocratic. Democracy is a public virtue, not the only one, and the relationship of democracy to other public virtues and vices can only be understood if democracy is clearly separated from other characteristics of political systems.

What is *liberalism*? *Liber*, as we know, means free in Latin. Liberalism has its roots in the freedom movements of the 18th century. It is an ideology that is critical of power and advocates openness, democracy, freedom and justice. This liberalism, sometimes called "classical," also wants a market economy and — this is usually forgotten — a small state.

If we marry the concepts together, we get a *liberal democracy*. It is a form of government in which it is not enough for politicians to be appointed by universal suffrage; society must also have constitutional freedoms: freedom of speech, assembly, religion and the press. Law is superior to politics, and everyone is equal before the law.

It is with this definition in mind that *Dagens Nyheter*'s editorial claims that Viktor Orbán, the EU's most democratic leader by the classic concept of democracy, is undemocratic. It is also this view that underlies leading Swedish politicians' claim that the Sweden Democrats are undemocratic, the political party that, at the time of writing, has the largest popular movement behind it.

When *Dagens Nyheter* writes that liberal democracy has been dismantled in Hungary, I think that Hungary must have an *illiberal* democracy. And that concept does exist. It was introduced in 1997 in an article in the American magazine *Foreign Affairs* when the diplomat Richard Holbrooke, just after the end of the war in Yugoslavia, wrote that an election may be openly called and properly conducted, but those whom the popular will brings to power can be racists, fascists and separatists openly opposed to peace and reintegration.

In fact, in 2014, Viktor Orbán himself defined his policies and Hungary's future as illiberal. He saw through the moralisation of the concept of democracy, i.e. that the term *liberal* stands for the multicultural, globalist and (actually) anti-democratic bureaucratic rule that Europe with the EU has ended up in. He was also old enough to see the kinship with the Soviet Union, which also governed its citizens by moral dictates. It is only just over thirty years since Hungary escaped Communism, and the Hungarians are clearly happy to have their country and culture back. They see how the EU is showing frightening similarities with the Communist Soviet Union.

## Alleged Anti-Semitism

In the local Swedish morning paper *Värmlands folkblad*, after the 2022 elections, one could read that Viktor Orbán, since he came to power in 2010, "successfully dismantled democracy" and that the Hungarian government is antisemitic, since it closed George Soros's Central European University in Budapest.[6]

Whenever criticism is directed at something Jewish, it seems always to be antisemitic in the eyes of the media. George Soros and his university were opposed not because of any antisemitic agenda, but because they are enemies of the traditional Hungarian society that Viktor Orbán wants to strengthen and maintain — the political

---

6    https://www.vf.se/2022/04/08/debatt-det-ungerska-valet-en-varningsklocka-for-oss-infor-valet-i-september/.

programme that he has a mandate from the people to implement. George Soros has no popular mandate and does not even live in Hungary. What he does have is all the money he has managed to accumulate in hedge funds and by gambling on various currencies, including the Swedish — clever, but hardly honourable.

## Population

There is another crucial political issue at stake here, one that is almost taboo in Sweden: not enough children are being born in Sweden to sustain the population. How should this problem be tackled? There are two major ways. Either, as is the EU's policy, we can fill the gap with immigrants, or, like Hungary, one can opt for a family policy that encourages citizens to have more children.

The Hungarian government has introduced a programme with the stated aim of increasing the number of Hungarian children born. Families with several children can obtain mortgages without having to pay interest. They can also get these loans if they commit to having at least three children. Women who give birth to four or more children are exempt from paying income tax for life. Families with children can get a grant of 8,000 euros to buy a car, but only if it has at least seven seats. These and other benefits introduced have resulted in a nearly 25% increase in childbearing over the past decade, from 1.25 to 1.55 children per woman.

The programme is not only about age structures and population pyramids, but it is also about Hungary remaining populated by Hungarians. There is thus a desire to preserve the Hungarian people.

For Swedish left-wing politicians and debaters, this is provocative. An editorial writer found it offensive "that the state is looking into the womb." She wrote that "rhetoric and policies that reward one's own people and exclude others should have no place in today's Europe." For her, such a policy was reminiscent of Nazi Germany.[7]

---

7    https://www.sydsvenskan.se/2019-02-11/nar-folk-blir-ett-fult-ord.

Social Democratic Social Security Minister Annika Strandhäll agreed, tweeting that these proposals "smack of the 1930s" and that Viktor Orbán "is creating blinders to what this kind of policy does to the independence women have fought for."

So what are these two left-wing feminists attacking? The answer is that Hungary's government, unlike Sweden's, has understood that the low birth rate is a demographic problem. It is not surprising that the Hungarian government reacted angrily and that Deputy Prime Minister Zstolt Semjen called minister Annika Strandhäll "a sick creature."

## Dishonest Comparisons

An analysis by Swedish Radio journalist Tomas Ramberg compares what he calls the double standards of the Left Party and the Sweden Democrats.[8] He goes back a bit in the history of the Left Party and writes that they "fought" for a long time for democratic rights in Sweden while excusing the oppression in countries like the Soviet Union and Cuba. Similarly, he argues, the Sweden Democrats are unreservedly democratic at home but deny "democratic restrictions" in Hungary and Poland.

I wonder how aware Tomas Ramberg is of the dishonesty of that comparison. The Soviet Union and Cuba were, and are, harsh dictatorships, while the political leaders in Hungary and Poland are appointed by the people in general elections. In other words, they are not undemocratic, although they do not support *liberal* democracy. We do not know whether Swedish voters do, because they have never had the chance to declare their opinion. Whether Sweden's politicians feel they do not need or do not have the courage to find out what the citizens think, I will leave unsaid. In any case, they will not be pitted against the wall by journalists like Tomas Ramberg.

---

8   https://sverigesradio.se/artikel/analys-ar-v-och-sd-hot-mot-demokratin.

On his blog, the conservative politician Sten Tolgfors, former Minister of Trade and Defence, writes that the Sweden Democrats are deliberately and consistently positioning themselves outside the liberal-democratic consensus shared by *the responsible* parties, which is enshrined in the Swedish constitution and on which democracy is based:

> Liberal democracy, also called constitutional democracy, is the form of democracy we have in Sweden and which the responsible parties, regardless of other starting points, have agreed should prevail in our country.
>
> Liberal democracy is an expression of the democratic system reflected in our constitution. The political conflict of the right-left scale has played out within this political framework. No responsible party has wanted to go outside it, the political price would have been very high.
>
> Liberal democracy is more than just an electoral system or a system of decision-making, it presupposes a set of values in society on which democracy is based. These democratic values are supported by and in our constitution.[9]

The Constitution contains a catalogue of rights and freedoms, together with the social ambitions and perspectives that Sten Tolgfors calls Swedish. Even if he does not write it in plain text, he means that multiculturalism is a Swedish value.

The Sweden Democrats, who define themselves as "a social conservative party with a nationalist outlook," disagree. In 2010, the Sweden Democrats voted against Sweden's reformed constitution, based on the constitution's views on multiculturalism, citizenship and Swedish EU membership. Thus, the Sweden Democrats have shown through political statements, party programmes and parliamentary action that the party's fundamental values are no different from those of the other parties in the Swedish parliament, which Sven Tolgfors calls *responsible*.

---

9   https://manskligsakerhet.se/2019/10/01/sa-avviker-sverigedemokraternas-varderingar/.

By unreservedly equating liberal democracy with democracy, Tolgfors opens the door to an essentially anti-democratic perspective. Sweden's ruling elite have enshrined their own values in the constitution, without consulting the people. Two acidic reflections in his own comment section:

> Please continue this stupid line against the Sweden Democrats and the party may get its own majority in the parliamentary elections.[10]

> And multiculturalism — what is it? Is it ok not to have to learn Swedish? To not have to follow Swedish laws and customs, for example regarding women's rights? That it's ok to wear niqab and burka in public places, like school? That it is ok for girls not to dress as they want, not to be outside the home after school and not to meet boys without a male relative present, or not to marry whom they want? Is this the kind of 'multiculturalism' that Tolgfors pines for? Or what does he mean? I guess his arguments are clichéd and 'politically correct.' How does he explain that almost 25% of all adult Swedes agree with SD? Does he mean that 1/4 of all Swedes […] are undemocratic?

The Sweden Democrats distinguish between liberal democracy and democracy, i.e. the opportunity for citizens to make their voices heard in general elections and referendums. When it comes to governing, the party is considered ultra-democratic. For them, the will of the people is almost sacred. Their party manifesto reads *"that all power in Sweden should emanate from the people is the most central of the Sweden Democrats' principles."* This makes them the opponents of liberal democracy.

## Human Rights

That all human beings are created equal, with inviolable rights, is one of the most central ideas of the Enlightenment. It led to both the US Declaration of Independence in 1776 and the French Revolution of

---

10  The Sweden Democrats won more than the Conservatives in the Autumn 2022 election.

1789 (liberty, equality, fraternity). Although it cannot be said to have been a guiding principle in the 19th century — accompanied, as we know, by both colonialism and the slave trade — it still remains an undercurrent in European thought.

In December 1948, the United Nations published its *Declaration of Human Rights* in Paris. The concept of liberal democracy henceforth becomes synonymous with a society that respects human rights. Something happens that not everyone understands. While democracy is a burden that the people want to place on their leaders, human rights is a demand that goes the other way. One can take the concept of asylum as an example. Without examining whether it has a popular response, the UN defines asylum as a human right. In our time, this will be interpreted in many Western countries as meaning that the people not only have an obligation to grant asylum to refugees but also to bear the costs associated with this, even when the asylum seekers have travelled halfway across the world to seek asylum, as is the case in Sweden. Thus, what was originally, and at its core, a non-political method of appointing and dismissing leaders, and of taking popular decisions on important issues, i.e. democracy, has been filled with both a financial obligation and a moral content, still without testing whether this is in accordance with the will of the people.

The UN Declaration of Human Rights has been elaborated in a total of thirty articles. The first is the 1948 founding document, the latest came into force in 2010 and is called the *Convention for the Protection of All Persons from Enforced Disappearance*. That wording sounds like it was taken from a satirical joke magazine.

In addition, there are several international conventions which have in common that they are neither popular nor particularly international. Going back to 5 August 1990, we find the *Cairo Declaration of Human Rights in Islam*. Muslims from all over the world, through no less than 45 foreign ministers, expressed their common position. The Declaration was intended to be an annex to the UN Declaration on Human Rights, but formally it has never been granted such status.

Nevertheless, it is an important declaration in that so many Muslim states have endorsed it. The two central articles are No. 24 and No. 25:

- All the rights and freedoms stipulated in this document are subject to Islamic Sharia.

- Islamic Sharia is the only reference for explanations and clarifications of the articles in this declaration.

Article 19 is also interesting in that it declares that no punishment shall be imposed other than those prescribed in Sharia. It should be acknowledged that the declaration establishes that women are the equal of men in terms of human dignity. Yet it is a void passage, since every Muslim knows that the Koran clearly states that God created man to be superior to woman. Equal rights for men and women do not apply. It is also hard to believe that the rights of LGBTQ people are affirmed in Muslim countries. Nor is it likely that they would improve if citizens were allowed to express their views in a referendum.

There is also a 2008 Arab Charter on Human Rights. It prohibits not only racism, but also Zionism. The reason is that the Arabs want to wipe out Israel. Consider the following in light of these facts: In 2009, the UN Human Rights Council passed a resolution stating that criticism of religion is prohibited.

Human rights is a political battlefield where different countries and geopolitical blocs disagree.

## What the World Should Look Like

On the Swedish government's website, under the heading *Democracy and Human Rights,* you can read the following introductory passage:

Human rights are universal and apply to everyone. They state that all human beings, regardless of country, culture and context, are born free and equal in dignity and rights.[11]

This is a deeply problematic formulation, firstly by stating an *obligation* that the state has, if it wants to call itself democratic, and secondly by claiming that people have rights that are universal, i.e. apply throughout the world. These are big words, given that human rights are not universal even within the UN's own domains.

The claim of human rights is *normative*, that is, this is perhaps how the world should be. But it is not, and it will never be. No human being is born free; we are all born into a specific social and economic situation. The children of a textile worker in Bangladesh have very different conditions from the children of a UN ambassador, even if the ambassador spends fourteen hours a day working on human rights issues. How could it be otherwise?

In this context, 'free' is a watchword without any connection to reality. It is possible to say that the countries that have signed the UN Declaration on Human Rights cannot allow slavery, but that is as far as the possibility of realising a universal concept of freedom goes.

It should also be said that rights, as a concept, are completely meaningless without specifying the context in which they apply. Anyone does not have the right to be in a housing queue or to receive social assistance in Sweden. No one has the right to be a judge in a court of law. No one has the right to go into a woman's dressing room. No one is simply allowed to play football in the Swedish national team. In short, what kind of generally valid rights does the government intend with its declaration?

---

11   https://www.regeringen.se/regeringens-politik/demokrati-och-manskliga-rattigheter/fakta-om-manskliga-rattigheter/vad-ar-manskliga-rattigheter.

## Values-Based Democracy

In 2015, journalist Marika Formgren put forward the concept of *val-ue-based democracy (Sw. Värdegrundsdemokrati)* as a kind of Swedish turbo version of liberal democracy. With the vision of an equal, femi-nist and cosmopolitan society that fights against all kinds of oppres-sion, the value-based democrats believe that they have expanded the domains of liberal democracy. These can be found on both the right and the left of the political scale. Marika Formgren writes:

> The Swedish democratic values are thus almost identical to the ideology of the Swedish post-Marxist left, minus specific views on how economic policy should be formulated. The question is how it got this way. How did the idea arise that democracy is not a form of popular government based on free debate, but a state in which all people share the post-Marxist views that constitute the "democratic value foundation?[12]

The value-based democrats' norm criticism presents itself as a propa-ganda that is oppressive and demanding in almost every possible context. Citizens are prohibited from using certain words; they are not allowed to be xenophobic, homophobic, or critical of Islam, and certainly should not adhere to any outdated gender roles. Officials are sent for training, and if they skip various propagandistic lectures (from the left activist think tank *Expo,* for example) there is a risk that it will be considered as misconduct.

This is where responsible citizens need to play their part. Journalists in particular must recognise their responsibility. The sup-posedly objective Swedish state broadcasting corporation SVT has made a brand out of democracy based on values. For example, when I listen to a programme on the success of Swedish gaming developers, the reporter must complain that it is not an equal arena. Women have

---

12   https://magasinetneo.se/artiklar/demokrater-for-asiktsfrihet-och-demokrater-emot/.

been held back for various reasons. Then a successful female player is interviewed.

Probably half of the times I turn on the radio, racism and anti-racism is one of the main themes, or in the very least is present on the side. It doesn't interest me, so I switch it off. If I'm in the car, I'll switch to another program. If that doesn't work either, I'll switch to a commercial channel. I would rather listen to commercials, where I'm sure the immune system works, than be trained to be another soldier of politically correct Sweden.

And when, for example, I think it is a completely ludicrous statement that all people have equal value, it is a very strong signal to the value-based Democrats that I am undemocratic. It does not matter that I affirm constitutional rights. Nor does it matter that I (and anyone else) can easily win an argument about people's equal worth. People who do not think that everyone has equal value are undemocratic, period!

What the value-based Democrats are doing is allowing an emotionally charged and identity-producing approach into the democratic framework. Argumentation becomes limitless and political concepts are transformed from having real content to becoming invectives. See, for example, the use of the terms fascism/neo-fascism in public discourse. An example below from a left-wing blogger (there are plenty of them):

> The Sweden Democrats are undoubtedly a fascist party with members who have nothing against violence. It is an undemocratic party that has no objection to changing the constitution in a negative undemocratic direction. For Sweden Democrats, all people do not have equal value. It is these beliefs that lead to terrorism and mass murder of the Breivik type, that lead to shootings and murders of immigrants as happened in Malmö with the serial shooter Peter Mangs.[13]

---

13  http://blog.zaramis.se/2012/08/26/det-odemokratiska-och-rasistiska-partiet-sverigedemokraterna/.

To continue with Marika Formgren, she writes that in the value-based Swedish democracy, sports clubs must profess these values in order to receive operating grants. Staff at various authorities are sent on special value-based training courses. In Sweden, the scandal is greater if the police "fail to uphold values" than if they fail to enforce the law. Managers responsible for serious mistakes are not asked questions by journalists about how and why, but about their values.

The value base is so vague that its adherents are constantly finding new "anti-democrats." If, instead of going on about values, local politicians sigh that the housing shortage and the burden of supply mean that Sweden cannot cope with the current volume of immigration, they are racists, and thus anti-democrats. The head of the budget who says that taxpayers should not pay for gender-neutral toilets is a "cis-normative anti-feminist," and thus an anti-democrat.

How did it get to be like this? Let's go back in time. When the Social Democrat Carlsson government made the decision on 13 December 1989 to stop immigration, there was hardly any thought that this might be undemocratic. What could be undemocratic about the country's government warding off a flood of asylum seekers who, by their sheer numbers, risked putting the country in a problematic state? This was the reasoning not only of the Social Democrats but also of the Moderates and the Centre Party.

The Liberal Party, the Green Party and the Left Party considered the decision undemocratic, expressing their discontent through protest. From their perspective, it was an irrelevant question whether the country was able to receive and take care of the asylum seekers.

The Conservative Party leader Carl Bildt reasoned in the same way when in May 1990, he was subjected to a half-hour-long grilling on television by the news-programme *Aktuellt*, just before the Moderates' party conference.

That time it was the Conservatives who were not considered fully democratic. The reason was that some forty proposals had been submitted to the meeting. They had in common that they were critical of the very high level of immigration due to the Balkan war.

A coalition of the centre right parties won the 1991 elections and Carl Bildt became Prime Minister. The Liberal Party and their leader Bengt Westerberg, classic valuebased democrats with whom by necessity Carl Bildt was allied, were given responsibility for Sweden´s immigration policy. Now Carl Bildt said nothing about basic democratic rights. Value-based Democracy had triumphed. Two decades later, in September 2020, the Swedish government published its guide *The State´s Value Base—Common Principles for Good Governance.* Among other things, you can read:

> The Swedish Agency for Youth and Civil Society (MUCF) denied a state grant to the Youth League of the Sweden Democrats (SDU) on the grounds that the organisation's activities did not respect the ideas of democracy. SDU appealed, but both the Administrative Court and the Court of Appeal concluded that no grant should be awarded. The courts held, among other things, that the SDU had not shown that the organisation met the requirement of respect for democratic ideas and that its programme of ideas contained generalising and negative statements about immigration and immigrants.[14]

---

14  https://www.statskontoret.se/publicerat/publikationer/publikationer/den-statliga-vardegrunden--gemensamma-principer-for-en-god-forvaltning/.

# More Immigrants?

## Low Birth Rates

ACCORDING TO Statistics Sweden, Sweden's population increased by a total of 1,289,397 people between 2002 and 2018. Of these, 902,106 were born in another country; 283,100 were born in Sweden with two parents born abroad; 214,120 had one parent born in Sweden and one born abroad. This makes a total of 1,399,326 people, but this does not include newborn children with two Sweden-born parents.

It's easy to get confused by high numbers, but look at them again. How is it that the number of inhabitants is higher before than after counting those who are children of native parents (here called Swedes for the sake of simplicity)?

The answer is that the Swedish population decreased by a total of 109,929 inhabitants during the period, partly due to emigration, but mainly because more people died than were born, i.e. a negative birthrate. In 2018 alone, the number of Swedes decreased by a total of 8,280 people; 3,850 left Sweden and the birth deficit was 4,430.

In 2020, 1.67 children were born per woman in Sweden. About 35% of them were non-European women who gave birth to between 2.24 and 2.98 children.[1] This means that — in contrast to Swedish women — they are comfortably above the limit for reproducing.

---

1   https://tobiashubinette.wordpress.com/category/icke-vita/page/18/.

For a population to be self-sustaining, the standard statistical number is 2.11. This is the average number of children each woman needs to give birth to in order for a population to survive. However, this figure is not set in stone. More and more women in Sweden are giving birth quite late in life. The oldest first-time mothers are in Stockholm County, where the average age in 2020 was 30.9 years. The youngest mothers in 2020 were in the county of Södermanland, where the average age of first-time mothers was 27.8 years. This makes the break-even point lower, at 1.9 children per woman.

This is not a measure that Sweden reaches either. The economic crisis around 2008/2009 led to a decline in childbirth and it has continued to fall since then. In 2020, Sweden's 1.67 children per woman put it in 131st place out of 197 countries.[2] This is higher than the EU average of 1.59, but not enough for the population to reproduce itself.

From 2000 to 2021, Sweden's population increased by more than 1.6 million, while the ethnic Swedish population decreased by almost 30,000. For those who believe that Sweden should remain the country of Swedes, the statistics are alarming, but the picture is much the same not only in Europe, but in the world's most urbanised countries in general. Childbirth is lower in southern Europe than in the Nordic countries. The lowest birth rates in Europe are in Italy, Spain and Malta.

The explanation for this is not only economic ups and downs, but also the way society is structured. One reason often mentioned is the possibility for women to combine work and family life. Childcare and parental insurance are less well developed in southern Europe, forcing many women to choose between having a career and having children.

Although the low birth rate is a demographic problem of the first order, there is no political interest in trying to get women in Sweden to have more children. Instead, those in power want to solve the issue

2   https://www.ui.se/landguiden/statistik/topplista/?factid=943dc176-04da-e511-9c3d-f01faf3e8f24&charttype=bar&countries=.

through migration. This of course raises the question: why? And the follow-up question: why don't Swedish women want to have more children?

## Childless Women

In Sweden, it is taken for granted that children are born when it is most convenient for one's career. In the well-educated middle class, this usually means that the mother is between thirty and thirty-five years old. One or two children is enough, because the parents must also manage their careers and secure their finances. Despite all the allowances and other benefits, having children is expensive.

In the fight for female emancipation and privilege, the male elite has allied itself with the elite women, who affirm the right to child restraint and the right to abortion. Duties are rarely discussed. In particular, there is no mention of the duty, in the interests of the nation, to have more children. Western and Swedish women do not want to give birth to many children, because it restricts women's freedom.

In Germany, 30% of all women are childless. Of German women with a university education, 40% are childless. This is not only true in Germany. President Macron of France was well aware of this when he said: "Show me a well-educated woman who has decided to have seven, eight or nine children."[3]

This long-range planning makes us unable to understand people who do not link childbearing to life careers. For example, it seems irresponsible for people living in poverty or in a situation where the future is still unresolved to give birth, especially if it happens repeatedly. We do not really understand why they just let it go on.

---

3   http://joh27cam94lou.bloggo.nu/Sverige-och-en-fri-invandring/.

## The Foundations of National Sovereignty

Alva and Gunnar Myrdal were the big stars of Swedish social debate in the 1930s-40s. One of the issues they highlighted was Sweden's birth rate, which had fallen sharply during the depression of the early 1930s and was the lowest in Europe. The winter of 1932/33 was a particularly difficult one, with one third of Sweden's children estimated to have been undernourished.

Alva and Gunnar Myrdal calculated that, if the trend was not halted, Sweden would have almost twice as many elderly as people of working age by the end of the 1970s. Something had to be done to get Swedes to give birth again. Families with children needed support. It was not just about child allowances, but about preferential housing loans, subsidised rents, free health care and free school meals. In other words, this is the foundation of "Folkhemmet" (The National Home).

The couple's most famous book, *Crisis in Population*, was published in 1934. Already on page 9, they write, proving to have a clearer understanding of the situation than today's politicians:

> The consequent decline in population would signify the degeneration of a race and "the suicide of the family." As population pressure was reduced, the country would be flooded with immigrants from foreign races with higher fertility rates. By right of the strong, these would take over and reshape our precious cultural heritage. This invasion could also bring international complications and endanger our peace. At the same time, the reduction in the number of children would weaken our defences and expose the country to predatory conquerors.

The Myrdals did exactly the opposite to the politicians of our time when the couple highlighted the risk of "Immigrants from foreign races with higher fertility rates." As we know, politicians today do not see immigration as a threat, but as an opportunity, especially when it comes to solving the demographic problem. To formulate oneself like Alva and Gunnar Myrdal has become impossible. For contemporary politicians, it is a perfect example of the racism that they consider necessary to fight, both across the board and in the long run.

Many of the Myrdals' ideas on how to boost childbearing were implemented. 1937 saw the introduction of the means-tested child allowance. The universal child benefit was delayed for another eleven years. Special apartment houses were built, where families with at least three children but poor finances could find good accommodation. In 1943, a state subsidy was given for preschools. The birth rate, which in 1935 was 1.8 children per woman, had risen to 2.7 ten years later.

## Immigration Is Not the Solution

Today, there is an ongoing population crisis, but no politicians or opinion leaders are sounding the alarm. Sweden has one of Europe's highest limits for free abortion, at week 18, and in some cases, after approval by the National Board of Health and Welfare, week 22. This is stunningly close to the limit at which a foetus can survive outside the mother's body. Most countries set the limit at week 12. Moreover, it is easy to get an abortion in Sweden, and the extremist feminist political party Feminist Initiative thinks that free abortion is so important that Sweden should offer it free of charge to women in other countries where abortion is not allowed. But not only that: everyone in Sweden under 21 years of age gets free contraception. The state's message is clear: enjoy your sex life but don't make children. Presumably, our feminist government thinks that the demographic deficit can be compensated for with mass immigration. But can it?

Demography is a hard science in the sense that it works with facts, and demographers say that maintaining the population through immigration does not work. Even if today's immigration were three times higher and all immigrants got jobs immediately at arrival, it would not solve the challenges of an ageing population.[4]

A report from the Nordregio research centre in 2016 clearly illustrates this.[5] The report calculates how much net migration is needed to keep the 2015 age structure constant in the future. As the average age rises over the period, this becomes difficult. It turns out that 38.1 million immigrants are needed in the period 2015 to 2080 to maintain the age structure that Sweden had in 2015. From 2080 onwards, annual immigration of about 1.5 million people is needed.

With so many immigrants a year, it is impossible to maintain national unity. Thus, immigration is not a realistic solution to child-bearing. Yet, immigration continues at a total of around 100,000 residence permits per year, despite politicians trying to present it as Sweden being at the EU's minimum level.

It may be added that the employment rate among immigrants, including young people, is so low that they do not constitute an economic asset, but rather become a burden on the taxpaying population. Importing unemployment will not make it any easier to pay future pensions.[6] Immigrant dependants are an additional burden on the system. An organisation called The Entrepreneurship Forum found in 2020 that of working-age migrants from the Middle East and Africa, only about a third reached a self-sufficiency level of 12,600 SEK net/month, which is the EU minimum.

Sustainable demographic development can only be achieved through the fertility of its own population. Immigration is not a solution but rather exacerbates the problem.

---

4   https://www.sydsvenskan.se/2015-04-10/sa-ser-invandringen-ut-i-din-kom-mun.

5   https://nordregio.org/staff/timothy-heleniak/.

6   https://www.youtube.com/watch?v=Rlk9aoZBzps.

## Dangerous Knowledge

It is not only the increase in population that is frightening, but also the number of people. Anyone interested in the intelligence of different populations is challenging one of the most cherished dogmas of our society: the equal value of all human beings. Somehow, equal value presupposes equality between people in other respects too, not least intelligence. Very many people believe in the claim "you can be anything you want to be." Even more people have the delusion that at birth a human being is like a blank slate, where anything can be written.

IQ is one of the most innate differences, and scientists have been measuring intelligence for over a hundred years. Scientifically, it is one of the most reliable areas of research.

In 2006, psychologist Richard Lynn and political scientist Tatu Vanhanen published their controversial report *IQ and Global Inequality*, in which they compiled IQ tests from different countries. For sub-Saharan Africa, they arrive at an IQ between 60 and 77 and an average for the region of 68. Another study from 2010, presented in the journal *Intelligence*, arrives at an average of 82. This is still far below the population average of 90 that is usually cited as necessary to build functioning democratic societies in the Western sense. Lynn and Vanhanen have also established a correlation between the average IQ of different countries and their GDP per capita in their report *IQ and the Wealth of Nations.*[7]

The US military requires a minimum IQ of 83 for employment. Two attempts have been made to lower this to 80 but these individuals could not learn soldiering skills well enough to justify the cost of additional training. Although no IQ figures are available, this also seems to apply to the Swedish armed forces. In July 2015, Dagens Nyheter reported that the armed forces' entrance exams, which "are

---

7    https://www.researchgate.net/publication/289962908_IQ_and_the_Wealth_of_
Nations.

designed to suit an 18-year-old Swedish-born, male population," are too difficult for too many immigrants.[8] To avoid being accused of discrimination, they therefore lowered the admission requirements.

This kind of "dangerous knowledge" leads into very important areas. Why did the people of the not very large island nation of England manage to subjugate a large part of the world in the 19th century? Was it something to do with British intelligence? Why did North America, unlike Mexico, manage to take over and develop a high-level civilisation in the 20th century? Did it have to do with Northern European thinking?

One of the most important political scientists to specialise in the rise and fall of civilisations, Samuel Huntington, asked in his last book *Who Are We?* (2005) if the US would have been the same US if instead of being ruled and dominated by the British, the country had been settled by French, Spanish, or Portuguese Catholics. The answer is no. It would have been Quebec, Mexico, or Brazil. Huntington noted that what he calls the Anglo-Protestant culture, a culture with the Protestant work ethic at its core, was a basic premise.

In *At Our Wits' End: Why We're Becoming Less Intelligent and What it Means for the Future*, Edward Dutton and Michael Woodley argue that between the 15th and mid-19th centuries, the richer half of the population in Europe had more surviving children than the poorer half. Since economic status and intelligence were positively correlated with the previous generation, this meant that people became increasingly clever with each new generation. The authors argue that the growth of intelligence was the basis for the Industrial Revolution, which brought us a wealth of inventions and a higher standard of living.

However, this process led to a shift in population growth from the richer to the poorer half. There are several reasons for this, but perhaps the most important was the dramatic reduction in child

---

8    https://www.dn.se/nyheter/sverige/forsvarets-antagningsprov-ar-svart-for-utlandsfodda/.

mortality. The rich stopped giving birth to many children, because they did not risk losing all their heirs. They could further raise their standard of living if they did not have so many children. For the poorer half, they do not have the same control over their lives. Even if they do not have as many children as before, they still have more children than the richer half.

In other words, those with lower intelligence started having more children than those with higher intelligence. This may be particularly true for women, since those with better conditions and higher intelligence acquire more advanced education and choose to postpone childbearing until after peak fertility, i.e. after age 30. Occupation comes first. Women in the poorer and more uneducated strata often have their first children in their teens.

## Muslim Fertility

There is another factor, which with the concept of Islamophobia is also taboo, namely what will be the consequence of the fact that so many of the migrants to Europe are Muslims? Even though Islam is the world's fastest-growing religion, and despite the fact that the experience worldwide is that Muslim migrants do not integrate into the culture of the host country, this must not be discussed in Sweden.

Of the people who are granted residence permits and give birth to more children than Swedes, the majority are Muslims. Muslim leaders have no problem understanding that, in the long run, this means that Muslims are taking over. For example, Turkish President Erdoğan has urged Muslims in Europe to have at least five children. But it doesn't take as many as five for this to be a quicker process than is generally understood. If 10% of the population is Muslim and 90% secularized Christian Europeans, it doesn't sound like it would be that demographically threatening. But if Europeans have a birth rate of 1.3 children per woman and the Muslim birth rate is 3.5, that means Muslims will catch up within two generations. This is not a racist or Islamophobic statement, but a statement based on facts.

From 2014 to 2017, 68% of all asylum seekers were male. The population increase in our country is largely made up of uneducated people, mostly young men, from the most violent and dysfunctional Third World countries (dominated, of course, by Islam). As much as 12% of Sweden's 21-year-old men were born in Afghanistan. The top countries in 2018 were:

1)  Syria

2)  Iraq

3)  Iran

4)  Georgia

5)  Eritrea

6)  Afghanistan

7)  Stateless

8)  Uzbekistan

9)  Somalia

10) Albania

The most common reason in 2018 was to immigrate as a relative of someone who held residency in Sweden: 61% of women and 35% of men gave this reason. In the group of family migrants, around four out of ten were relatives of previously immigrated refugees. Almost half of them were Syrian citizens. The figure for family migration is in fact higher, but neither bridal imports from the countries of origin (new relationships) nor those relatives arriving after more than two years are recorded in the Migration Agency's statistics.

According to estimates by the US think-tank Pew Forum, Sweden's population, with such high levels of immigration as occurred between 2014 and 2016, could be 30.6% Muslim by 2050.[9] This is twice the average for Europe in the same year. Only two countries in Europe will have a higher percentage: France, due to immigration from the former colonies, and Bulgaria, where a large part of the population is Muslim since ancient times.

Finnish systems analyst Kyösti Tarvainen has repeatedly tried to warn the Swedish Parliament that if immigration is not drastically cut, Sweden will have a Muslim majority in the foreseeable future, with all that this implies. The facts he presents show that this is completely irrefutable and a total disaster for everything that Sweden stands for. In an email to me, he writes: "I sent my calculation to all members of parliament in Sweden. I have been sending similar reports for five years in a row. No one answered, except a Social Democrat who wrote back: "Why do you write in English when Swedish is an official language in Finland?"

The political elite dismisses this kind of reasoning as racist, even though it is of crucial importance for Sweden's future.

---

9   https://www.pewresearch.org/religion/2017/11/29/europes-growing-muslim-population/.

# Another Story

## Mankind's Primordial Home

A T THE risk of assuming that there may yet be or have been some societies that do not have a story about themselves, I would argue that all societies have just that: glorifying tales about themselves. The Western world's greatest origin story is, of course, the Biblical story of Genesis, of Adam and Eve. Like the latter, most stories paint a picture of a lost golden age, a paradisal origin.

In 1544, the chronicler Johannes Magnus demonstrated that Sweden had a history that stretched all the way back to the year 88 after the Flood (year 2259 BC).[1] Magog was the name of the first Swedish king. Other kings mentioned are Sigge II, Hunding, Frode, and five different Björns. Our current king is known as Carl XVI Gustaf, but it would have been more correct to use Carl X Gustaf, since the first six probably never existed. Erik XIV should have been called Erik VIII. There have been many king Karls and king Eriks responsible for shaping Sweden's long and consequential history.

Another track, which doesn't really contradict the fantastically improbably list of kings cited above royal length, is *Gothicism*. It claims that the Swedes are descended from the Goths who ravaged the Roman Empire during the dark centuries. It was a happy time, and the Goths were heroes. Since the Middle Ages, and especially

---

1    Johannes Magnus, *Historia de omnibus Gothorum Sveonomque regibus* (1544).

during the Swedish Great Power era, this was the most cherished myth of origin.

During the 18th century, this myth faded, though it did not die. After Sweden lost Finland to Russia in the war of 1808–09, it gained new momentum. When it soon became clear that the interest in Goths was exhausted, they were replaced by Vikings. For example, Viking helmets with horns were invented, for which there is no archaeological evidence. The word *Viking* is found on a few rune stones and seems to mean something like "pirate." It was not the name of a people or a group. Most people stayed on the land. They were not pirates, but rather lived a peaceful life as livestock keepers and farmers.

In the 17th century, the creative polymath Olof Rudbeck the Elder launched *The Atlantic,* an alternative narrative. Sweden was in fact the sunken Atlantis and thus the home of all humanity. Rudbeck lined up a lot of hilarious "evidence" to "prove" that this was the case. Among other things, Eve got her name because Adam was so surprised when he saw her that he said "Eh, what?!" ("*E va?*" in Swedish). The Peloponnesus was named after a guy called "Pelle på Näset" and Hercules came from the Swedish name "Härkalle." The Visigoths and Ostrogoths originated from the landscapes Väster- and Östergötland and the Cimbris from the town of Simrishamn.

## Mass Formation Psychosis

It's strange, isn't it, that people can believe this stuff? A good explanation is given in a nearly 90-minute conversation between Belgian psychologist Mattias Desmet and American philosopher Aubrey Marcus.[2] They discuss the question of whether a population can be mass hypnotised. Unsurprisingly, the answer is that not only can it be done, but that it happens repeatedly.

There are several terms that refer to what is happening: mass psychosis, groupthink, brainwashing, collective hypnosis, etc. What is

---

2    https://www.youtube.com/watch?v=IqPJiM5Ir3A.

being used in this conversation is *mass formation psychosis*. It can be associated with how one formats a hard drive so that it can be loaded with the right software for the tasks one wants it to perform.

It's not that the smartest are harder to convince in a mass-formatting process. It affects all kinds of groups. This was the case in both the Soviet Union and Nazi Germany. We don't know what it is that distinguishes the category of people who see the consequences and retain their reason and capacity for logical thinking.

Approximately 30% of the population subjected to this mass formation is hypnotised. Around 40% of the population follows this first group because they do not want to go against the conventional wisdom. It is both difficult and too dangerous. The remaining 30% of people resist. If this last group manages to put forward its protests strongly enough to take the lead, then the 40% group goes with them. Then the tide turns, the fish shoal turns back into a school, and the hypnosis is over — if Belgian psychologist Mattias Desmet is to be believed.

One difference between mass formation psychosis and hypnosis is that in hypnosis the hypnotist never hypnotises himself, whereas mass formation psychosis affects large numbers of susceptible, suggestible, people. There is not always a hypnotist, as it is often a self-directed process. On the other hand, the process of formation produces strong leaders who have the power to legitimise the necessary rituals and carry out the required actions.

## The Power of Narrative

For me to move forward in this reasoning, I need a common and unifying narrative for a collective that answers the question of life's true meaning. However, there is a problem with the term "narrative," namely that it is too passive. The unifying narrative is not only a story but above all a call to fight *Evil* and *the Evil Ones*, which can look very different in different narratives. It is suspenseful when one "discovers" that there is some kind of enemy that must be attacked and defeated. Mass formation psychosis always creates new victims, because there is anxiety and a sense of futility behind it.

The important thing here is to understand that this is a fight that can never be won, because the fight itself is a pseudo-phenomenon. What it's all about is identity building. The unifying narrative shows what needs to be done to make life meaningful. There are studies showing that Londoners experienced the Blitz as the happiest time in their lives. They really felt that there were strong ties binding them together, even though houses were collapsing and people were dying. It is for the same reason that people don't commit suicide when they must endure extremely difficult conditions. In the Gulag, according to Solzhenitsyn, people did not take their own lives. When strong external danger threatens, people unite and focus on survival. Life becomes meaningful and then people don't commit suicide.

That the narrative of The Other, the evil ones, can lead to genocide, has happened many times in human history. The paramount one is, of course, the Second World War and the Holocaust.

The narrative can have such a strong hold on the hypnotised that they even kill their own. It attacks logical thought, reason, and even self-preservation. The witch hunts of the 17th century are a frightening example. In some Swiss villages the fight against the evil Satan went so far that there were almost no women left at all. Both women and men became extremely focused on the task at hand, blind to the consequences, as well as blind to the suffering they were orchestrating as they burned alive the women who had previously been their neighbours and close friends. Sweden, too, suffered. During nine years in the 17th century, over 300 women were executed for witchcraft.

The three greatest genocides of the 20th century took place in Stalin's Soviet Union, Hitler's Nazi Germany, and Mao's China. As many as 15% of the most loyal communists in the Soviet Union were executed in the 1930s without disturbing the people's worship of

Stalin. Something similar happened in 1945 when Germany stepped up the murder of Jews. Contrary to what one might think, it was then that resistance among German dissidents was at its weakest. During Mao's "Great Leap" in 1958–62, an estimated 45 million people died. Most were beaten, starved, or forced to work themselves to death. Neither Stalin, Hitler, nor Mao were deposed by their own people, whom they subjected to murder and mass death. The fact that all three remained in power until their deaths tells us something about how a narrative can maintain power.

## To Belong to the Collective

In contemporary Sweden, the state controls the approved narrative and the media promotes it. The media is the hypnotic voice. There is also media coordination: all major media follow the same script; the press, state television, and radio and commercial channels. To this can be added the authorities that have already been formatted: the church, the armed forces, preschools, schools, universities. And not least the newcomer: social media, where, thankfully, there is also a strong opposition. Left-liberal ideologies do not cope very well with public opinion.

For mass formation psychosis to be unleashed, there needs to be widespread dissatisfaction and a large and free-floating anxiety. If people feel that their lives lack meaning, there is an anxiety, which they can't really anchor to specific societal problems. They don't know why they feel the way they do. That this is the case can be seen, for example, in the huge amount of sleeping pills and antidepressants that are prescribed. According to the World Health Organization (WHO), this condition is so widespread that it affects one in five people. Free-floating anxiety is a painful condition.

The state of anxiety also contains a free-flowing aggressiveness. You don't really know why you are upset and aggressive and so you look for something to connect with that can put an end to the conditions you think you can discern. It could be the oppressive patriarchy, the racists, or the climate deniers.

Now the stage is set for a new story, a narrative which can be disseminated through the mass media, and which points to the reason for the miserable state in which one finds oneself. By formatting oneself according to this narrative, one is doing something that will improve the lives of all people. Thus, media provides these disgruntled, disillusioned, depressed, aggressive people with a strategy. As a leader of the Christian Democrats said when he supported immigration and a generous refugee policy: "What is the meaning of life if you are not allowed to be good?"

By believing in a narrative and joining the fight, people feel they are back on track. They feel a meaningful connection. There is a new solidarity, new social ties, a new meaning to life. This is why people believe in the narrative and join the strategy set out by the media, however absurd. It is important to understand the reason why they affirm both the narrative and what needs to be done. It has nothing to do with reason and credibility but is the response to a psychological crisis condition. Media consumers are given a social bond shared with other people, a story that is affirmed and with which it is "right" to show solidarity.

Humans are social creatures and being socially isolated is painful as well as real. They switch from being socially unattached to having community and the feeling that now life works, a feeling that is confirmed by the collective.

## Progress

During the period of 20th-century modernism, Sweden was given a narrative that turned its gaze from the greatness of the past to the possibilities of the future. It was the West's great story of progress, which Sweden unreservedly embraced. "The world's most modern country" was a well-known designation picked up in 2006 by a very popular domestic television series.

Progress becomes the measure of time, and not only Sweden and the Swedes but all of humanity move towards ever greater perfection. In the light of modernity, the golden myths of the pre-industrial era become fool's gold, and history is reduced to events and technology that are inferior to those offered by modern society. Knowing the major features of Swedish history will no longer be part of general education. This lack of history manifests itself in everything from a lack of interest in Swedish history in general to indifference to the various periods of literature, the massive wanton murder of thousands of historic listed buildings in all 290 Swedish municipalities between the 1950s and the 1970s, and a deafening lack of interest in one's own roots and genealogy.

I am convinced that many Swedish teenagers today do not know their grandparents' names, where they came from, or what they did for a living. Such things are considered unfashionable and nerdy. Even if it is not said outright, there is a perception that our ancestors were less intelligent than people today. They didn't know as much as we do, and, because they were deeply religious, they didn't think logically and rationally either. Conventional wisdom says that our time is the best time, and yet it will be even better in the future.

Material progress becomes both the grand narrative and the norm of modernity. Children no longer learn the names of Swedish kings, but car models. Or mobile phones. They become consumer savvy. Who wants an older car or phone if you can get the latest and greatest model?

Ultimately, faith in the future is a religious idea that paints the future in utopian shades and distorts the view of history. We are on the way to the perfected and liberated human being. The myth of progress is the myth of human independence and self-sufficiency.

## A Global Control Society

In the early '90s, the Finnish-Swedish philosopher G. H. von Wright wrote *The Myth of Progress*.[3] He argued that the development of modern society was unsustainable. After two world wars and the Holocaust, this narrative has lost its grip. Science and technology, which had been such a boon to men and made their lives easier, was about to become man's greatest enemy. Von Wright warned that progress was running amok.

Three decades later, this fear in the form of digital technology has made a frightening contact with reality. It's not just about almost all of humanity being hypnotised by mobile phones and living more of their lives online, but also about the emergence of a global control society. The world's population is divided into two categories: the obedient and the disobedient. The latter are punished and have their lives curtailed in various ways.

A global computerised register of the world's population could be linked to reward and control systems of the kind we already observe in China. For the Beijing regime, it is a pipe dream come true, they call it "harmonious." For the less compliant citizens, this vision of the future looks more like a nightmare.

Without being given a choice, the Chinese are provided with a digital account with a starting amount of one thousand points. If they behave, associate with the right men and consume the right things, they accrue more points. The digital account is also linked to membership of various dating sites and millions of street cameras with facial recognition. High plus points provide a host of benefits, discounts and travel opportunities. Those who don't pay their bills on time, walk against red traffic lights, associate with inappropriate people, or are critical of the regime, get minus points.

---

3    G.H. von Wright, *Mycket om framsteget* (1994).

The story of the future is being transformed by new digital technologies from a utopian tale of liberation to a dystopian tale that puts Orwell's *1984* to shame.

## The Fight Against Oppression

Two stories are outdated. The one that romanticises the past, as well as the one that idealises the future. Truth, reason, logic and grounding are central concepts in modernity's bright story of the future. That may be so, but two world wars speak for themselves. A new narrative is needed.

The story of postmodernism has a completely different approach. It claims that all truths are relative and prioritises the fight against oppression. What von Wright is saying, and which becomes even clearer during the rise of postmodernism, is that if progress is dead, anything goes. This means that the lie is also permitted and is placed on the same level as the truth. What is truth no one can know. Speech no longer serves as the tool of truth, and besides, who cares? It is even the case that "truth" appears as one of several ideological constructs. Logical reasoning does not trump ideological thinking. Reason does not prevail over emotion.

The new rhetoric highlights neither the Swedish people nor the homeland. For the left, it is no longer a question of fighting the bourgeoisie and capitalism; anti-racism becomes the main struggle, and "xenophobia" the main target, to be followed by the struggle against the patriarchal white man, who was the creator of the society that should now be consigned to the graveyard.

## Rebirth

While modernism has one big story, postmodernism has many smaller ones. The narrative launched by Sweden's political class is Sweden as a *humanitarian superpower*. With the multicultural decision in 1975, Sweden took the step from being a country in Scandinavia to becoming a country in the world. Although Social Democratic Prime Minister Olof Palme himself never seems to have used either the term moral or humanitarian superpower, he was the godfather of the new political outlook. Olof Palme's policy is not compatible with the idea of "The National Home," a very powerful political concept.

Olof Palme put forward the opposite thesis, that revolt and discontent have always been the driving force forward, towards a better society. He therefore vociferously opposed apartheid policies, communist rule in Czechoslovakia and Franco's military dictatorship. When he sided with North Vietnam in the Vietnam War, it did not seem to bother him that North Vietnam was a totalitarian one-party state like the Soviet Union and China. Coercion camps, purges and liquidations were not mentioned.

The North Vietnamese were fully aware that the war was largely played out in Western media. As the professor at Lund University Inger Enkvist notes, Sweden became perhaps North Vietnam's main propagandist in the West:

> There was a "barter trade": the Vietnamese got their propaganda out and also received substantial aid from Sweden, and Swedish diplomats and politicians could enjoy a grandiose self-image. Can we see the same trend today? For example, could the treatment of unaccompanied minor refugees, who cannot prove their age, have been influenced by the desire of leading politicians to enjoy a grandiose self-image?[4]

Olof Palme also criticised the way the superpowers treated developing countries and welcomed thousands of political refugees to Sweden in the 1970s. He supported the one-party state of Tanzania, praised Fidel Castro and kept quiet about the genocide in Cambodia. Under Pol Pot's leadership between 1975 and 1979, the Khmer Rouge orchestrated their vision; they would impose complete, classless

---

4   https://www.svd.se/a/Qo2rJJ/viljan-att-gora-sverige-till-moralisk-stormakt.

communism in one fell swoop. Perhaps that is why they renamed the country Kampuchea. The cities symbolised capitalism and intellectual, well-educated resistance. That's why the cities were emptied of inhabitants. They were ruthlessly driven out into the countryside to work in agriculture and irrigation.[5]

Out of Cambodia's population of 8 million, about 2 million were killed. Anyone with glasses was executed because it was a sign of being intellectual. Half of all the country's children were orphaned.

There are 23 countries that have tried communist ideology, all of which have failed. Today, apart from China, there are only four states that claim to be communist: North Korea, Cuba, Laos, and Vietnam. In addition, there is one country that is still de facto a communist state: Belarus. None of these countries can serve as a model in any political context. North Korea is a country that we alternate between describing as one of the most brainwashed dictatorships to have ever existed and a dangerous military power that repeatedly threatens the world.

However, there is a crucial paradox: communism, while totally collapsing as a political reality, has mutated and gained steam as a system of thought. Communism may have lost the world, but like the phoenix, it has risen from the ashes and reconquered the intelligence of the West. In a modernised form, it totally dominates Sweden.

When the tabloid *Expressen* "revealed" in 1994 that IKEA founder Ingvar Kamprad had been a Nazi during World War II as a 17-year-old, Kamprad immediately apologised, explaining that this was youthful folly. A lot was written about this, even in obituaries about him after his death. This is what *Expressen* wrote: *He married twice, had 4 children, and is accused of being a Nazi.*

The very popular Swedish actor Sven Wollter was never confronted in the same way, even though in many contexts he said that he was

---

5    https://www.so-rummet.se/fakta-artiklar/roda-khmererna-och-folkmordet-i-kambodja.

proud to be a communist. In 2014, he said in an interview in *Dagens Nyheter*:

> I'm a communist, and don't come throwing that Joseph Stalin stuff in my face. I have read Joseph Stalin, and there is much in his writings that is right, even if he made some mistakes at the end.[6]

Until his death, Sven Wollter was a member of the Swedish Communist Party, which has Stalin on the wall of its premises. And we heard these neutral words of remembrance from Prime Minister Stefan Löfven after Sven Wollter's death: "As faithful as he was to his art, he was equally devoted to his political ideals."

Imagine if Ingvar Kamprad had said, "I'm a Nazi and damn proud of it. Don't come throwing that Hitler stuff in my face. I've read Adolf Hitler, and there's a lot in his writings that's right, even if towards the end he made some mistakes," and then happily continued to be part of a party with Hitler framed on the wall.

Had he gotten away with it? Hardly! No matter how successful IKEA had been, Kamprad was to become persona non grata in the Swedish public sphere.

As sensitive as the Swedish journalist profession is to what is perceived as "right-wing extremism," it is just as insensitively blind to left-wing extremism. With gender education, aggressive feminism, mass immigration, and multiculturalism, the new Swede is to be created. Everything on the public stage is controlled by left-wing liberals. They dictate the terms of business, they control politics and bureaucracy, they debate in the media, they write the books, they create the arts, they dominate among teachers, among musicians, among dancers and daycare workers. Everywhere!

6   https://www.dn.se/kultur-noje/wollter-slang-inte-stalin-i-fejset-pa-mig/.

## The Fight Against Apartheid

In a long and very informative article, journalist Bengt G. Nilsson says that Palme became not only a poster boy for the Vietnamese Viet Cong guerrillas, but for guerrilla movements all over the world. He associated with Fidel Castro and became an idol in the non-aligned movement. It was during Palme's time as prime minister that Sweden developed very extensive and largely secret support for liberation movements in Africa.[7]

The Social Democrats wanted to fight against apartheid and invested over 2 billion SEK, which was channelled to the South African resistance movement in all sorts of strange ways, including through secret bank accounts in Switzerland. In an interview, author and Swedish Literary Academy member Per Wästberg talks about how Swedish aid funds were channelled to the opposition in South Africa via agents and secret channels. He himself smuggled in tens of millions of kronor in aid to political prisoners and their families and to lawyers who could defend them.

In addition to smuggling in money, various legitimate projects in South Africa were used as cover. An art gallery could receive money which was then channelled to people in the resistance.

It is not clear how much Swedish money was channelled to South Africa in total. One figure mentioned is 2.5 billion SEK in government funds alone. In addition, churches, trade unions, and other non-profit organisations raised large sums. Per Wästberg talks about how they constantly had willing smugglers, such as benevolent radical upper class people. They also had funds in Swiss banks under false names like "Freedom from hunger" and "Freedom from hardship."[8]

It was Sweden's right and duty to react and to try to help abolish the system because South Africa was violating the UN Charter's

7  https://timbro.se/smedjan/i-sverige-har-gerillan-alltid-har-ratt/.
8  https://www.dn.se/nyheter/sverige/sverige-skankte-miljoner-till-anc-i-hemlighet/.

requirement for equal treatment of people, regardless of racial and ethnic origin. All in all, almost 10 billion SEK in aid was probably channelled to the African armed communist liberation movements where Sweden, often secretly, provided "humanitarian" support while the Soviets supplied the movements with weapons.[9]

Former prime minister Ingvar Carlsson, Palme's successor, far more involved than he was, has proudly talked about this support. But isn't this criminal? To my knowledge, no one in a position of responsibility has said that this was outright theft from Swedish tax payers. Nor has anyone demanded that these politicians be brought to justice.

As we all know, things have not gone well for the ANC. Today, when we sit with the facts, it is not so obvious what is a good political act, but that is not the main reason why the Swedish support is outrageous. The question that should hurt and not just be brushed aside is with what legitimacy the Swedish government supported a resistance movement on the other side of the world and even did so illegally. Note that we are talking about the Swedish government, not any independent group.

## It Reeks of Self-Righteousness

In 1986, Social Democrat Pierre Schori declared that Sweden should be a humanitarian superpower. Eleven years later, as Minister for Migration, he talked about the challenge of harnessing the rich offerings of diversity. He stressed how important it was for Sweden to be an open society where different cultures, languages, traditions and religions were represented. Never again would Sweden become "a closed and isolated country with an internal life that is independent

---

9   Bengt G. Nilsson, *I tyst samförstånd: Sverige och Sovjet i kalla krigets Afrika* (Ethnopress, 2017).

of the outside world."[10] As if Sweden had ever been such a country. At the end of this speech in the Swedish parliament, he also said something quite astonishing. Those who question immigration policy were to be criminalised and hunted down: "In a democracy, it is not possible to find excuses, for example that immigration and refugee policy is wrong."

I am amazed that the opposition let this pass. The only thing that happened was that some critics sneeringly commented that "The Parliament is apparently a club for mutual admiration, which literally reeks of self-righteousness and political correctness."[11]

That's a good observation; political correctness is popular with the power elite because it transforms power into authority and turns propositions about the world into descriptive or implicit truths.

The new rhetoric of the Social Democrats had found its form, where one should particularly observe how the concept of democracy is brought into a new context. Sweden "is in a global landscape" and anyone who is "racist" is also undemocratic.

A few months later that year, a unanimous Parliament adopted a bill from the Social Democratic government entitled *Sweden, its Future and Diversity*. It called for multiculturalism to be realised "with massive propaganda efforts."

The wording *propaganda efforts* makes me cringe. It is downright frightening that neither the government nor the Parliament understood what propaganda is.

## Begging for Forgiveness

There are two leading Swedish politicians who have distinguished themselves by their ardent desire to play a role in world politics. The first, of course, is Olof Palme. The other is Conservative Party leader

10  https://www.riksdagen.se/sv/dokument-lagar/dokument/protokoll/riksdagens-snabbprotokoll-199697106-onsdagen_GK09106/html.

11  http://www.bgf.nu/schori/riksdag/schori.html.

Carl Bildt (prime minister 1991–94). In 2010 when he was Minister of Foreign Affairs he was called "a medium sized dog with big dog attitude" by the US Embassy in Stockholm in 2010. Three years later, in his Foreign Policy Declaration, Carl Bildt pointed to Sweden as a humanitarian superpower.

In 2012, Sweden was the world's third largest national humanitarian aid donor, funding humanitarian efforts to the tune of more than 5 billion SEK. Carl Bildt was proud that Swedish aid helped people in need in all major crises throughout the world.

And of course, even internationally, Swedish aid is impressive. Not five, but more than 50 billion kronor — 1% of gross domestic product — is distributed each year.[12]

Two years later, in a bizarre and suicidal speech that probably helped his government lose the general election of 2014, then moderate prime minister Fredrik Reinfeldt repeated that Sweden should be a humanitarian superpower. He also said:

> I want to remind you that we are a nation that has stood up and been open in the past in times when people have endured hardship. We now have people fleeing in numbers similar to what we had during the Balkan crisis in the early 1990s. Now I appeal to the Swedish people for patience, to open your hearts to see people in strong stress with threats to their own lives fleeing, fleeing towards Europe, fleeing towards freedom, fleeing towards better conditions.[13]

Reinfeldt was praised by the Social Democratic editorial writer Lena Mellin of the tabloid *Aftonbladet*, who began by stating that it will be a strain on the whole of society to receive so many people, many of whom are also quite broken after terrible hardships. It was a political kiss of death when she unreservedly praised him for not even trying to hide the fact that opening the borders to refugees would be both a difficult and expensive undertaking.

---

12   The conservative government that came to power in 2022 has cut the aid budget to 0.9% of GDP.

13   https://sv.wikipedia.org/wiki/%C3%96ppna_era_hj%C3%A4rtan.

Then it was time for a Social Democrat, Margot Wallström, to take over the foreign policy helm. By now, the self-congratulatory image of Sweden as a humanitarian superpower was so well established that it was time to take another step. Soon after she took office, Margot Wallström proclaimed that Sweden was the world's first government with a feminist foreign policy. An editorial in the conservative morning paper *Svenska Dagbladet* commented that the Foreign Ministry had become a home for wishful thinking, a desire to improve the world.

On 4 July 2020, no less than 233 social democratic commentators wrote in *Aftonbladet* that Sweden should be a humanitarian superpower. Most of them were unknown to the public, but, unsurprisingly, the former minister Pierre Schori was there too. The text was a mindless and mechanical enumeration of phrases: humanity, human rights, the equal value of human beings, international conventions; almost a record of bottomlessly embarrassing conformism. For several years the Social Democrats had taken this image of Sweden as a humanitarian superpower very seriously, identifying with it one hundred percent, using it without any reservation or the slightest ironic distance, since it was considered to express what the leader Olof Palme created.[14]

Elected officials live in their own world — estranged from the people they are elected to represent. To them, all welfare immigrants are refugees, multiculturalism is enriching and everyone who claims to be a child from Afghanistan is, of course, one. There, Islam is the religion of peace and there is no difference between ethnic Swedes and Swedish citizens. There, all immigrants long to work "with eager hands" in the Swedish elderly care system, or at least to be integrated. The postmodern struggle is for an equal society, and the most important weapons are democracy, feminism, human rights, anti-nationalism, anti-racism and — in the case of Sweden — the values base.

---

14  https://janolofbengtsson.com/2020/07/07/socialdemokratisk-skamloshet/.

## Inverted Narratives

Modernism's grand narrative is replaced by postmodernism's many smaller narratives. What is going on in our time is a desperate search for a new unifying narrative, but we are not there yet. What we have today are several limited narratives, often owned by a country's power elite, but unable to convince a large enough majority of citizens. There are three major stories. Although not big enough themselves, the risk is that they will be fused together into one dominant narrative, resulting in a totalitarian state:

- Patriarchy and feminism. Women are still fighting for *equality* with men, even though they already have it. The fight will then be about *equal outcomes* and ultimately about who should have power in society, men or women. It is not that this struggle is ever won, but that the struggle leads from legitimate demands to pathology. For the victors, winning would be tantamount to being thrown back into futility.

- Globalism, which is partly about anti-racism and partly a fight against nationalism. National leaders who have the people with them in the defence of their own country are called undemocratic. Pathology is very much about political rhetoric. What must not be said and what must not be touched? Which words and narratives are forbidden, and which are allowed?

- The fight for the climate, which is the story with the strongest religious overtones. At the first UN environmental conference in Stockholm in 1972, the organiser, who became the first head of the UN Environment Programme, warned that the world had only ten years to avoid disaster. In 2004, the British *Guardian* newspaper wrote that unless drastic action was taken, climate change would wipe out civilisation by 2020. Major European cities would sink below sea level. A "Siberian" climate and violent riots awaited Britain. Nuclear war was likely to follow in the wake of widespread drought and famine.

Swedish Television's climate journalist Erika Bjerström is one of those who has contributed greatly to the fact that many people in Sweden, especially children and young people, are anxious about the climate threat and believe that climate change in ten years' time will lead to the end of the world. In her 2019 New Year's speech, she said:

> As we toast 2020, we have exactly ten years to break the downward emissions curves. 2020 is also the year that the world's countries will announce their increased ambitions at the next climate summit, then in Glasgow. It is still possible to curb runaway warming with "immediate and drastic action" according to IPCC scientist Hoesung Lee.[15]

Exactly ten years? How on earth could you know such a thing? Erika Bjerström should have learned from previous doomsday prophets. Neither the Maldives nor Manhattan is now under water as they should be, according to the IPCC's projections and guesses. And we always seem to have ten years before disaster strikes.

Despite 50 years of predictions that have been completely wrong, climate activists, journalists, and politicians are still successfully selling the image of imminent doom, and unfounded fear-mongering has real consequences. Young people around the world are suffering from climate anxiety.

The narratives of postmodernism are *inverted*. If men spontaneously tend to become leaders, politics must favour women. If women naturally take care of children, then policy must force men to be with children. This is why "daddy months" (paternity leave) is an important goal in Swedish politics. If people are naturally heterosexual, then the allocation system must put everyone but the heterosexuals first. If one group rules and another is subordinate, then

---

15 https://www.svt.se/nyheter/utrikes/analys-nar-vi-sager-adjo-till-2019-kan-vi-se-tillbaka-pa-det-varmaste-decenniet-sen-matningarna-inleddes.

the subordinate is oppressed. Minorities take precedence over the majority.

We are the biggest and strongest, but also the worst, so we must make amends. It is not our enemies who must be defeated, but we must defeat ourselves. Particularly white men with power must refrain from using their strength because they hurt other people.

Basically, society is responsible for the shortcomings of its citizens. It is the task of those in power to distribute and compensate, thus promoting greater justice. Those who are unable to cope on their own are supported by the state, while the strong are to be held back by the same state. In post-modern society, this has come to apply to politically weak groups. Ethnic and sexual minorities are highlighted: look, here are the oppressed groups that society must help and support! Minority groups who have never taken even rudimentary responsibility for the common society are rewarded with extraordinary and costly efforts, for the sole reason that they are considered oppressed. This also applies to groups that are severely criminalised and do great harm. Inversion is the tool that will produce justice.

## The Same Old Totalitarian Spree

Nothing says that the new paradigm is better than the old one. On the contrary, we recognise this quest for equality not only as one of the most important tasks of democratic society, but also as something that has brought societies to ruin in the past. The prime example, of course, is communism. The heroes who would lead us to the classless and just paradise were, in reality, some of the most terrifying and genocidal maniacs in world history: Lenin, Stalin, and Mao. What good is it that this beautiful story has cost so many millions of lives? More than 170 million people have been killed in mass murder in the 20th century. That's about four times more than those who have died on the battlefields.

# Heroes

## The Principle of Innocence

MULTICULTURAL SWEDEN needs a new set of heroes. They must have done something for the world, and preferably they must have done it by helping an oppressed group. The most oppressed group of all is, of course, the Jews.

Gone are the revered kings, gone are the much-admired inventors and engineers of modernity. Three new names are Raoul Wallenberg, Folke Bernadotte and the greatest of them all, Dag Hammarskjöld. The hero who led the world until his death in 1961 was Swedish!

Barbro Hedvall, a long-time editorial writer for *Dagens Nyheter*, had this in mind when she wrote in March 2022:

> The humanitarian superpower — that's how we've wanted to see Sweden during my adult life. That great power, like its predecessor, has its heroes, a Raoul Wallenberg, a Dag Hammarskjöld, a Harald Edelstam. Helpers in danger, saviours in need in Budapest, at UN headquarters, in Santiago de Chile. And many have come: from the white buses of 1945...[1]

I'm mulling over that "we" for a while. The popular anchoring is missing. These are the heroes of the upper class, the elite — those who have honourably strengthened the story of Sweden that the official Sweden wants to show the world.

---

1 https://www.dn.se/ledare/barbro-hedvall-stamningarna-som-skapade-den-humanitara-stormakten-sverige-lever/.

Most Swedes who have been around for a few years know who Dag Hammarskjöld was, but he was certainly no man of the people. He was the son of a Swedish prime minister, whose place in the Nobel Prize-awarding Swedish Academy he inherited from his father.

As a person, he was a highly gifted and sophisticated humanist. On long flights between war zones, he is said to have relaxed by translating French poetry. Less flattering, but also true, is that he was a humourless asexual mystic. Throughout his life he struggled with his belief in God. Among other things, he had a meditation room set up in the UN skyscraper in New York.

When his plane was shot down on its way to a peace brokerage mission in republic of the Congo in 1961, it seems he had foreseen his own death. In his home he had left a farewell letter and a manuscript, *Markings*, published in 1963, after he was posthumously awarded the Nobel Peace Prize.

Hammarskjöld's path to power was a bit surprising. Although he was a professor of economics, his academic career was rather undistinguished. The fact that he did not wear academic dress when he got his doctorate probably attracted more attention than the thesis. When he got the "world's most impossible job," he was the fifth UN candidate after the Soviets refused to accept the four previously proposed. It was a surprise to most observers that Hammarskjöld got the job. World leaders probably did not really know who this low-key and unpolitical figure was. He seemed to have no career aspirations.

The appointment was logical, an application of the principle of insignificance. The politician who is strong and pushes issues risks a fight with many belligerent opponents and competitors. So, it is wise to avoid this. Action is a quality that is secondary to conflict avoidance.

Superpowers like the Soviet Union and strong countries like Germany do not want competition from supranational organisations. The major nations make sure that a representative but rather dull and cautious leader is elected, without a strong profile — a sympathetic person who lets everyone have their say, creates dialogue, holds meetings, listens to everyone, sets up working groups, works on diversity, makes study visits, investigates and adopts resolutions, and starts projects that rarely lead to anything concrete and forward-moving.

The UN headquarters is in New York, not in the seat of power, Washington. The fact that the EU is in Brussels is hardly a coincidence. It could not be placed in a strong country like Britain, Germany, France or Italy. Even the Netherlands was a bit too cocky and independent. Belgium was just anonymous.

Many may know the names of the current UN and EU leaders (Antonio Guterres and Ursula von der Leyen), but how many can point to anything politically significant they have achieved? They participate in countless talks and conferences but who cares? They are basically bureaucrats.

There is no denying that Hammarskjöld was a successful leader, even if he was not the world leader he was hailed as in Sweden. His greatest achievement was probably his mediation of the Suez Crisis in 1956 and forming a peacekeeping force from neutral countries. Another was the two conferences he organised in Geneva for the disarmament of nuclear weapons.

## Black Carnation

Barbro Hedvall omits Folke Bernadotte. This is no coincidence, as I shall return to. Instead, Harald Edelstam takes his place among the heroes. The only thing one might readily associate him with is that he is supposed to have somehow saved Chileans when Augusto Pinochet came to power in 1973.

Edelstam also came from the upper class. This did not prevent him from being politically on the left, which should have guaranteed his place in eternity, at least for the Social Democrats.

After saving hundreds of Norwegian resistance fighters and Jews during World War II, he became known as the Black Pimpernel, a reference to the "Scarlet Pimpernel." To the Norwegians, he was a hero. It was also thanks to Edelstam that thousands of Chileans came to Sweden as political refugees when Pinochet seized power. Wikipedia tell us that:

> The most spectacular operation took place when he managed to rescue 54 Uruguayans from the National Stadium who would have been executed the following day. [...] The new regime did not appreciate the engagement, and expelled Edelstam after a fight between the Swedish embassy staff and Chilean military when a sick asylum-seeking woman was abducted by Chilean military. According to Wilhelm Wachtmeister, Director of the Swedish Foreign Ministry, this was not entirely unwelcome to the Swedish government, which saw itself relieved of the "necessity of recalling him." On 4 December 1973, he was declared "persona non grata."[2]

A biography of Harald Edelstam has been written, entitled *The Black Pimpernel*. The Swedish actors Michael Nyqvist and Mikael Persbrandt have portrayed him on screen. There is also a foundation that awards a prize in his memory to people who have made contributions requiring great moral courage. Harald Edelstam undoubtedly meets the standards of a Swedish hero.

It turns out that he was not the compliant person suitable for politics. In an article in the evening newspaper *Expressen*, one of his sons tells of how his father was praised upon his return from Chile:

> My brother Hans was there when Harald arrived like a madman, hooting and hollering, wrapped in a big Chilean flag. The whole crowd cheered and the flashbulbs went off. Hans happened to be standing next to one of Harald's bosses, then cabinet secretary Sverker Åström. Hans said that the more the very excited Harald crowed, the more bitter Åström looked.[3]

---

2    https://sv.wikipedia.org/wiki/Harald_Edelstam.

3    https://www.expressen.se/debatt/pappa-raddade-liv--blev-mobbad-pa-ud/.

At the Foreign Ministry, Harald Edelstam was not at all popular. The only one who supported him was his own older brother, Axel, who was also an ambassador and in the leadership. What was not to everyone's liking was that Harald Edelstam spoke to journalists and did not always stick to protocol. As the *Expressen* article reads, "His prejudiced colleagues at the time would probably at most have helped some drunken guest at a cocktail party."

On the other hand, he had, at least for a time, the government with him, in particular Olof Palme. But the government also betrayed him. He had expected a post in Europe, after his many years in Asia and Latin America. That was not to be. Foreign Minister Sven Andersson, with some vague excuses, kicked him out to the periphery, to Algeria.

What should I conclude from this? Possibly that it is not enough to be a hero "for real" to be celebrated by the Swedish power elite. My hypothesis is that Swedish Social Democrats are happy to forget about Harald Edelstam, not because he doesn't measure up but because they don't.

## Famous and Forgotten

Raoul Wallenberg is the world's most celebrated, famous and forgotten Swede. That he is forgotten is based, among other things, on the twelve videos about Raoul Wallenberg that are available on YouTube. The one with the most downloads is when President Obama honoured him in 2014. It has just over than 27,000 views. The clip showing Ronald Reagan making Raoul Wallenberg an honorary citizen of the United States in 1981 has less than 4,000 views. Only two people in modern times have received this honour. The other is Winston Churchill. Since then, Wallenberg has also been made an honorary citizen of Canada, Hungary, and Australia. Israel has named him one of the *Righteous Among the Nations*, a distinction that guarantees him a place in paradise. As recently as 2012 he, or his survivors, were awarded a gold medal by the US Congress.

There are streets, squares, schools, and other institutions named after Wallenberg. He even has a special day (27 August). And the works of art are manifold: he has a bronze portfolio outside the UN-building in New York which can also be found at his birthplace, on Lidingö outside Stockholm. The house itself, however, burned down many years ago.

Have there been films made? Yes, several. Theatre? Yes, even an opera by the Estonian composer Erkki-Sven Tüür.

## A Letter Arrived

Without a doubt, Raoul Wallenberg was a true hero. In 1944–45, he saved many thousands of Jews from the Nazi extermination machine. The Swedish legation in Budapest, of which he was in charge, issued so-called protection passports certifying that the holder was a citizen of neutral Sweden. The idea was the brainchild of Swedish ambassador, Ivar Danielsson, but it was Wallenberg and his colleagues, along with diplomat Per Anger, who implemented the rescue operation on a large scale. Without concern for his own safety, Wallenberg and his driver Vilmos Langfelder went to train stations, ghettos and other assembly points and ordered the release of Jews on his lists of protection pass holders. The lists were often made up or expanded on the spot, all to save as many Jews as possible. Many of those rescued were taken to buildings purporting to be Swedish territory. Wallenberg and his associates were not alone in this. The Swiss and some South American embassies also made an admirable effort.

This rescue operation could probably only be carried out towards the end of the war, when the Germans were in retreat. US President Franklin D. Roosevelt also played a role, in that he warned Hungary's head of state, Miklós Horthy, that he would be put on trial after the war if he obstructed the rescue operations.

When the Soviet army captured Budapest in January 1945, Wallenberg received a letter from a Red Army officer who wanted to see him. He did not know why. Wallenberg, then 32, was captured and taken with his driver to Moscow. They just disappeared. Most evidence suggests that the Russians suspected Raoul Wallenberg of being an American spy. It is likely that he was executed in 1947, but this is not proven. His official date of death is 31 July 1952, that is five years after he was last known to be alive.

## A Tool in the Cold War

In the 1970s, Wallenberg's fame took off. For American politicians, Wallenberg became a very useful symbol, the link that connected the Holocaust to the struggle between the US and the Soviets. After all, it was not the Nazis but the Red Army that kidnapped Wallenberg.

President Jimmy Carter was the first to recognize Raoul Wallenberg, describing him as a very interesting person and, furthermore, questioning why more was not known about him. Carter more or less campaigned for Wallenberg as one of the truly great heroes of World War II and the Holocaust. Interest in the Holocaust also grew strongly in the wake of the American TV series *Holocaust*.

But even the Americans did nothing special to free Wallenberg. They didn't really care about Wallenberg as a person. What mattered was that he was useful as a tool of the Cold War. His fate showed that the Soviets were no better than the Nazis.

Then Swedish politicians also got involved. The government's shameful inaction, when they could have done something, was consigned to history and Wallenberg could contribute to the promotion of Sweden. On the one hand, he showed that Sweden actually did something honourable during the Second World War. But moreover, he fitted hand in glove with the multicultural ideal, a true globalist! And best of all, he was not really a war hero but a peace hero. So, in both US and Sweden, he became a mythological figure — a hero of multiculturalism.

## "Take the Jews Last"

One hero that Hedvall does not include is Folke Bernadotte and his efforts to save refugees from Germany's concentration camps with the "white buses" at the end of the war. For a long time, this was seen as Sweden's greatest humanitarian effort of all during the Second World War, and after the end of the war, the white buses almost took on the character of a national monument.

Why didn't Barbro Hedvall let the Swedish count take his place among his nation's pantheon of heroes? The explanation is given in a radio documentary made by journalist Bosse Lindquist in 1998 with the very enlightening title *Take the Jews Last*. The film showed that the heroic story of the white buses was rather complicated, and that Folke Bernadotte was too questionable a character to be considered one of the great Swedish heroes of the Second World War.

## Cultured and Charming

In February 1945, Folke Bernadotte flew to Berlin to organise a rescue operation for war refugees in German concentration camps. The first to be rescued were "Swedish women with German connections living in the Third Reich." They were to be rounded up and driven to Sweden.

Bernadotte quickly got on speaking terms with Heinrich Himmler's closest man, the cultured and charming head of the SS intelligence service, Walter Schellenberg. In Bernadotte he saw a person who could offer two things, help in negotiating with the Allies and help in avoiding punishment after the war. He therefore did his best to see that Bernadotte's wishes were fulfilled.

At the first meeting with the German Red Cross, Folke Bernadotte arranged for German-Swedes living in Germany to be rounded up and driven to Sweden. One of the first to go was then 17-year-old Vera Oredsson. She was a member of the female equivalent of the Hitler Youth and would become the leader of the Nazi Nordic National Party as an adult.

According to the first meeting held in Berlin, the Jews were to be picked up last. This instruction came from the Swedish Foreign Ministry. The Jews in question were ordinary Danish and Norwegian citizens. This directive explains why they were not included at all in the lists of Scandinavians that the Germans allowed to board the white buses. Only three Scandinavian Jews managed to get on. To the last, the expedition leaders pushed to go to Theresienstadt in Czechoslovakia, where all 424 Danish Jews were located. The Norwegian Jews had been taken to Auschwitz and were almost all executed.

The reason was that SS General Walter Schellenberg had warned Bernadotte against trying to retrieve the Danish Jews in Theresienstadt. This could endanger the return of the other Scandinavians. The Swedish Foreign Office also forbade the trip, which was considered too dangerous.

However, it was urgent because Hitler had ordered that all concentration camp prisoners be killed before Germany admitted defeat. The gas chambers were to be dismantled and all witnesses wiped out before the Allies reached them.

The Danish representatives of the expedition then decided to circumvent Bernadotte. The Danish expedition member Johannes Holm bribed the Gestapo with a sumptuous dinner of Danish delicacies and plenty of booze. As a result, he received approval to carry out his mission (even without the consent of Folke Bernadotte and the Swedish government).

While the refugees were ferried to Sweden, Walter Schellenberg was flown to Sweden by the Red Cross in early May, along with other

SS men, their girlfriends and secretaries. He first stayed for a while in Folke Bernadotte's residence in Stockholm, where he helped Folke Bernadotte to write a book about his mission. It was published on 1 June 1945 with the title *The End: My Humanitarian Negotiations in Germany in the Spring of 1945 and their Political Consequences.* There are many indications that the publisher's editor, Ragnar Svanström, also actively helped to write the book. It received a mixed reception. Historian Folke Schimanski wrote in *Svenska Dagbladet* that Folke Bernadotte created his own legend without giving any credit to others. This did not prevent the book from becoming an international success, being translated into 18 languages and appearing as a series in the *Daily Telegraph.* Folke Bernadotte was now world-famous. British Stockholm correspondent Ralph Hewins saw two possible candidates for the leadership of a future United States of Europe: Winston Churchill and Folke Bernadotte.

Walter Schellenberg was later handed over to the Americans and sentenced at Nuremberg to six years' imprisonment for killing prisoners of war. It didn't help that Folke Bernadotte went there and testified that Schellenberg was a gentleman of the "old school."

In 1956, the Swedish Foreign Ministry published a White Paper confirming that the first phase of the evacuation applied only to Scandinavians, but that from 27 March 1945, Bernadotte could, if he thought it suitable and it did not compromise his mission to evacuate Scandinavians, also evacuate a number of Jews.

## Unforgivable Sorting

It is obvious why Folke Bernadotte was evicted from the heroes' gallery. Although it was in fact the Swedish government, and in particular the Foreign Ministry, that guided his mission, his friendliness towards Germany and his good contacts with the Nazis weren't in his favour. It seems unforgivable that the refugees were sorted out, even though it was at least partly for tactical reasons. First Swedes, then

Scandinavians, then French, Dutch, and Belgians. Preferably not Poles and other Eastern Europeans, and lastly Jews, whatever their nationality.

I would still like to see Folke Bernadotte as a hero. There is no getting away from the fact that he saved many thousands of lives. However, that is not enough for official and multicultural Sweden. The "Jews last" thing brings him over to the evil side. So get rid of him!

# A Multicultural Heritage

## New Heroes

THE DENIAL of Swedish history has itself become a Swedish tradition. In June 1997, the government gave the central cultural heritage institutions the task of carrying out special operations against xenophobia and racism. An annual appropriation of 1 million SEK was set aside for the preparation of new exhibitions, an inventory what earlier was done in this area. and training for museum staff. This work was based on a report prepared by the National History Museum on behalf of the Government. The authors of the report claimed to analyse the hidden, unconscious and unintended messages in museums' exhibitions, as well as the relationship between attitudes in society and interpretations of cultural heritage.[1]

The purpose of this mission was to increase public knowledge and understanding of these issues, and to raise awareness among cultural heritage institutions of how cultural heritage can and has been misused.

It became necessary to apply rhetoric which emphasised the equal value of everyone, a denial of both the Swedish cultural heritage and the cultures of various minorities. Even Muslims were claimed to be just the same as everyone else. The half-dead legislation on hate speech was polished up and politicised as a weapon against those

---

1   "Knowledge as power. How museums can counteract xenophobia and racism through their work." DS 1996:74.

who claim that Sweden is the land of Swedes and that all other ethnic groups can go where the pepper grows. Criticism of the political
establishment was misinterpreted as racism. And racism is of course
forbidden, not only as an act but also as an opinion. When a new party was formed, the Swedish Party, they were declared Nazis. The same
applies to the more successful Sweden Democrats. The most ardent in
this hate rhetoric was and is the party that has both Nazi and fascist
roots (Social Democrat Prime Minister Per Albin Hansson admired
and corresponded with Mussolini, to give an example of things that
belong to forgotten history).

Politicians must also learn to think differently about the Swedish
nation. The fatherland is being transformed from something belonging to the Swedes into a container that politicians can fill with more
people from all over the world. Ultimately, it was the parliamentary
decision of 1975 that allowed Sweden to grant 2 million residence permits in the first two decades of the new millennium. It is very reveal-
ing of how politicians and those in power think about Sweden when
Fredrik Reinfeldt, the conservative prime minister, in a discussion
triggered by a demographer who was out of touch with reality, agreed
that Sweden needed 38 million new inhabitants. As Dick Erixon, an
opinion leader, writes:

> Reinfeldt is an example of the unrealistic utopianism that is rampant in
> the establishment. Despite the complete failure of integration for 30 years,
> Reinfeldt believes in calculations that require new arrivals to be put to
> work immediately. How can such nonsense be peddled? No sensible
> person believes it. And that Sweden would accept one million migrants a
> year for 40 years… How is one's common sense, if one believes that the
> Swedish people would agree to that?[2]

---

2    Government Bill 1997/98:16.

# No Common History

The strongest bond between a country's citizens, the one that assures them that they belong together, is the nation's history. In Sweden, however, citizens' knowledge of history is astonishingly weak and almost never relevant to today's society. This is especially true for Swedes who went to school from the 1970s onwards. It is therefore interesting to read a government bill from 1997, which states in all seriousness not only that the Swedish people lack a common history, but also that this is not an important issue:

> The history of a country often acts as a unifying link between people. Since a large group of people originate from another country, the Swedish population lacks a common history. Contemporary belonging in Sweden and support for the fundamental values of the community are therefore more important for integration than a common historical origin.[3]

Did the authors understand what they were really proposing: that since Sweden has had significant immigration in modern times, we should cut our historic roots? Away with Engelbrekt, away with Gustav Vasa, away with Sweden's, long national history. This is probably also the political background to the following statement by the Social Democrat Mona Sahlin, later party leader, widely circulated online. In a speech to a Turkish cultural association, said:

> I think that's part of what makes Swedes so jealous of immigrant groups. You have a culture, a history, something that binds you together. And what do we have? We have Midsummer and all that nonsense.[4]

Mona Sahlin is not the only party leader to despise and deny Swedish culture. In 2006, Fredrik Reinfeldt, after a visit to immigrant-dominated Ronna in Södertälje, uttered his winged invective: "The pure

---

3   Government Bill 1997/98:16.
4   Turkish Youth Association's newspaper *Euroturk*, March 2002.

Swedish culture was basically barbarian. The rest of the development has come from outside."[5]

In an editorial from 2012, former DN editor-in-chief Hans Bergström shows a very different insight, but note that he doesn't go back very far either:

> Living abroad makes you more patriotic about Sweden. The observation is simple but not trivial. For me, the pride is above all in Sweden as "The Land of Innovation" — a country of engineers, inventors, scientists and entrepreneurs who broke new ground and fearlessly set out into the world. Even in the post-war era, there is much to be proud of, from Per-Ingvar Brånemark's titanium implants to Wirsbo's underfloor heating, Kamprad's furniture logistics to Rausing's milk packaging, Lars Leksell's beam knife to Niklas Zennström's Skype. Sweden is also attracting interest with social innovations, such as the new pension system.[6]

Since the Swedish export industry, which is the foundation of the Swedish prosperity, largely builds its success on domestic inventions, the only reasonable conclusion is that Fredrik Reinfeldt was talking in his night cap. The question is why he did so. Was it because he actually believed that this was the case? The term "barbarian" belongs to ancient Greece and was a derogatory term for all people who did not speak Greek. In contemporary Sweden, the term "barbarian" in the vocabulary of a prime minister is particularly offensive. If you call a people "barbarians," you are not only implying that they are primitive but also heartless and cruel. So, it is not a very honourable reference for a prime minister to use the term. What he said can be summarized simply as contempt for the Swedish people.

The excuse could possibly be that the Swedish school has ensured that neither Fredrik Reinfeldt nor Mona Sahlin know much about Swedish history. With their statements they only demonstrate their appalling ignorance — and that in their role as leading politicians.

---

5    http://www.dn.se/nyheter/politik/reinfeldt-det-ursvenska-ar-blott-barbari/.

6    http://www.dn.se/ledare/kolumner/varda-sveriges-framgangar/.

Among others, political scientist Olof Petersson has noted how ignorance and a lack of humanistic education are prominent in the political debate:

> The international outlook is usually absent. The experiences of other countries are noted with, at best, suspicious, often condescending interest. Sweden has been described as a constitutionally underdeveloped country. The constitutional debate suffers from a lack of awareness of its own country's historical traditions.[7]

## The Homogeneous Social Ideal

In 2013, an anthology entitled *Disrupting Homogeneity* (Sw. *Att störa homogenitet*) was released. It was part of a project of the same name that was carried out in close cooperation with the governmental commission for "Equal Representation in Museums," which had been developing methods for an LGBTQ+ perspective in the museum sector for several years.

According to editor Anna Furumark, the project *Disrupting Homogeneity* aimed to "break down notions of cultural purity and homogeneity as a social ideal." A transgender person opened the conference with a bass voice, skirt, and high heels. The presentation reads:

> That cultural heritage and history are among the most powerful political tools available is shown in a new way in the book *Disrupting Homogeneity*. The book provides a unique insight into how racism, Islamophobia, anti-Semitism, homophobia, funkophobia, and anti-feminism, all draw power from ideas of cultural homogeneity where the cultural heritage is used to divide people into those who are allowed in and those who are left out. The book suggests how we can appreciate the disruption of imagined

---

7    Olof Petersson, *Grundlagsändringar* (in Svensk *Författningspolitik*), ed. Ingvar Mattson & Olof Petersson (SNS 2011), p. 297.

homogeneity and in so doing create communities that include and bridge differences.[8]

Ethnologist and lecturer Britt-Inger Lundqvist summarises:

> The homogeneous society fears what is different, and it doesn't matter if it's travellers, Roma, Sami, LGBT people or anyone else who deviates from the mainstream norm. Disrupting Homogeneity has some 40 local and national partners working nationwide to deliver conferences and training. The aim is not only to disrupt homogeneity in the cultural sphere, but to cover as much of the public sector as possible. In the 10–12 conferences held so far, nearly two thousand people have participated. They include politicians, directors-general, governors and employees at various levels in social services, psychiatry and health care. They have listened to everyone from professors to transgender people, anti-racists and various norm critics. In addition, Education Radio has filmed selected conferences for broadcast. A look at some of the project's various programme items bears witness to the tale:

- Ideology of homogeneity

- Language as a tool for exclusion and inclusion

- Cultural heritage and xenophobic rhetoric

- Queer stories

- Estimate the disturbances

- The gender-binary city

- Disrupting homogeneity

- Ableism

- Local anti-racism[9]

Since, according to one of the speakers, we "float around in existence like eternal tourists," homogeneity is only a myth, a notion in the

---

8   https://nordicacademicpress.se/product/att-stora-homogenitet/.

9   http://cabam-cabam.blogspot.com/2017/04/min-text-i-boken-att-stora-ho-mogenitet.html.

eye of the beholder, a desire for a belonging that does not exist and never has existed. The "diversity resistance" must be broken down, as it is rooted in a pre-2000 position that the past consisted of a unified Swedish people with a common culture that "marched right through history." It is necessary to deconstruct the "cultural infrastructure of the past."

The above newspeak is richly sprinkled with attacks on the Sweden Democrats, which is paradoxical given that the party was democratically elected to Parliament. The organisers had the municipality and county council behind them and cooperated with a government mission. In general, government support at various levels was a prerequisite for the project to be run.

For example, the transperson and first speaker was a business developer at the Norrbotten Rights Centre. Under the motto "For diversity, against discrimination," this rights centre cooperated with the Anti-discrimination Ombudsman and other anti-discrimination agencies around the country. The Norrbotten Rights Centre is in turn part of the Christian study association Sensus, which highlights "life issues, diversity and global issues" and "offers the innovative meeting place, where people strengthen their skills, dare to transcend their boundaries and move their perspectives into the future." Another example is the Swedish Arts Council, which was represented in the anthology by its then Director General Kenneth Johansson. He asked how it was that 20% of the population in his home municipality voted for the Sweden Democrats.

The message from the government-funded project *Disrupting Homogeneity* was the need for a set of values that disrupt homogeneous society and the thinking that organisers believe homogeneity carries with it. By extension, homogeneity was said to lead to a chauvinistic and exclusionary nationalism, which carries xenophobia and racism in its womb. This in turn leads on to fascism and Nazism, with the ultimate goals of Auschwitz and Utöya.

## An Anti-National Museum

The Museum of World Culture in Gothenburg opened its doors in 2004, a Social Democratic project in which the then Minister of Culture, Marita Ulvskog, was the driving force. The large, beautiful and very lavish building was awarded Sweden's most prestigious architectural prize, the Kasper Salin Prize.

In English, the museum is called the National Museum of World Culture, which should be interpreted as meaning that the museum is not affiliated with any particular culture or academic discipline. But perhaps the most remarkable thing is that, unlike other museums, which celebrate and highlight something they are proud of, the Museum of World Culture is in denial. It is an *anti-national* museum.

Seven years earlier, the investigator, Social Democrat Lars Engqvist, had written in his report *Forum for World Culture* that the concept of world culture contributes to increasing diversity in Swedish cultural life, especially with expressions from countries and environments that do not reach their audience in Sweden through established commercial or institutional channels. Folk music from Senegal, artful coffins from Madagascar, face masks from Bali and Minoan drinking customs could not quite hold their own in the competition.

In addition, he argued that there was a "Swedish" cultural heritage that did not consist of log cabins with turf roofs, landscape costumes and folk music. Swedish citizens who were born in other countries, or had their roots there, were considered to have the same right as ethnic Swedes to have their cultural heritage affirmed.

The museum stated a few value words at the time: *engaging, exploring, inclusive, transnational* and *empowering*. About its activities it wrote: "The Museum of World Culture is a meeting place with thought-provoking exhibitions and activities on current issues in the world. Enjoy culture and good food in a great environment."

Many beautiful words and "home cooking from all corners of the world." But otherwise, you didn't really know what to do at the museum. What to exhibit was a bit vague. For a long time, the result was that the museum halls were largely empty. By 2016, the situation had reached the point where the management planned to rent out parts of the museum to an external tenant.

Unfortunately, it proved not so easy to keep to the politically correct lingua. Since the state was in charge, the state ideologues here had opportunities to do as they pleased quite more and differently than in the country's older museums. Or to do away with what they didn't want, which is what happened when the photo artist Elisabeth Ohlson Wallin's controversial picture sequence about LGBTQ people in Jerusalem was stopped in 2010. In one image, two naked men lie on the ground kissing at the Old Wall near the Jaffa Gate. A quote from the Bible is projected on the wall above the men. An image showing Muslims in prayer proved even more provocative. As for why this happened, the answer might be found in Islam's world of ideas, where images are often problematic.

The museum had contact with the Sweden's Muslim Youth organisation. They were very upset, and the museum management backed down. It was not the first time; five years earlier, after receiving threats, the management had taken down a painting by the artist Loulza Darabi, depicting a sexual act against a backdrop of a quote from the Koran.

At that time, the Swedish cultural elite reacted strongly. "The World Culture museum prostrates before rigid Muslims," wrote Agneta Klingspor in *Expressen*. "Up with the blackboard," wrote Jimmy Fredriksson in the evening paper *GT*'s editorial. I wonder if they would have been as cocky today, given the Muslim terrorist acts and riots that have occurred since.

## Voices from the Borderlands

In 2007, the Museum of World Culture in Gothenburg merged with three Stockholm museums, the Museum of Ethnography, the Museum of Far Eastern Antiquities, and the Mediterranean Museum. They were placed under a new authority called the National Museums of World Culture, based in Gothenburg. The authority was subordinated to the Ministry of Culture and was given a superintendent who was to manage all four museums. Instead of museum directors and curators, new staff members were appointed, but without specialist knowledge of the collections. As the costs of running the museums had soared, many knowledgeable curators were weeded out.

The first paragraph of the instructions for the National Museums of World Culture reads as follows:

> The mission of the State Museums of World Culture is to show and bring to life the cultures of the world. It shall promote interdisciplinary art education and public activities in new forms from ethnographic, archaeological, artistic, art-scientific and other social and historical perspectives. The Agency shall document and illuminate the manifestations and conditions of different cultures and cultural encounters historically and in contemporary society.[10]

Note the plural form, world culture is *many* cultures. The grand and fundamentally evolutionist and Western narrative delivered by white middle-aged men with hegemonic power is passing into history and being replaced by the postmodern stage where many narratives are being delivered. The concept of world cultures is *postmodern*. It is about the previously silenced voices of the borderlands making themselves heard. Now, people of every imaginable colour and gender would not only be objects but also subjects of the museum activity.

---

10   https://www.varldskulturmuseerna.se/om-varldskulturmuseerna/var-vision/.

For small countries like Sweden, there was a lot of international prestige to be gained if Sweden managed to be at the forefront of embracing the diversified society. It was argued that Swedes could be justifiably proud to be supporters of borderlessness and multicultural ideals.

## Strengthening Multicultural Tolerance

For more than a decade, cultural journalist Ola Wong had been writing about Asia, and China in particular, for the morning paper Svenska Dagbladet. His journalism was awarded several prizes. After eleven years living in Shanghai and Beijing, he moved home to Sweden and when he discovered what had happened to the Museum of Far Eastern Antiquities, he was horrified. They have one of the world's finest collections. Much of the catalogue was brought to Sweden in collaboration between Chinese and Swedish archaeologists; without these collections, there would certainly not be an East Asian museum in Sweden.

The museum had shifted its focus to "migration, integration, democracy and human creativity." The collections seemed to be of negligible interest. Now it was up to the State Museums of World Culture, and the director appointed by the Minister of Culture to "strengthen tolerance for multiculturalism."[11] The museum directors had been abolished, and the politicos had taken over.

Ola Wong wrote that the curator-in-chief wanted to cull the collections of the Museum of Far Eastern Antiquities and turn it into "an irrelevant PR agency for happy-clappy multiculturalism." It was disgusting that the government was turning Sweden's museums into propaganda centres. The Museum of Far Eastern Antiquities' biggest box office success was when it displayed the Chinese Terracotta warriors in 2010. However, that was not the exhibition that the

11   http://cabam-cabam.blogspot.com/2017/04/min-text-i-boken-att-stora-ho-mogenitet.html.

curator-in-chief was celebrating. She preferred the Silk Road exhibition, which grossly misrepresented Tang China as a model of female leadership and multiculturalism.[12]

Ola Wong received support from several journalists who agreed that what was going on was a politicisation of Sweden's museums. The Minister of Culture responded a week later with an article in *Svenska Dagbladet* in which she claimed that Ola Wong had misunderstood. On the contrary, it was important to cut ties with the collections to prevent ideological control of the content of the activities. The desire to merge the museums was due to high premises costs.

Now, three very knowledgeable anthropologists from the Ethnographic Museum entered the debate. They unreservedly sided with Ola Wong and wrote in *Svenska Dagbladet* that the high rents were a sham. There was money for the museums' activities, but it was eaten up by the market rents charged. It was the same taxpayers' money that was swirling around in the administration. They also pointed out how, year after year, all three museums had reduced their scientific staff, their conservators and their museum technicians.[13]

As Ola Wong sarcastically observed, the quest for diversity can easily lead to monotony. He was also interested in what was happening at other museums and wrote that in 2015, a gender strategist worked for eight months to teach the staff norm critique at the new Performing Arts Museum on Östermalm in Stockholm. When the same museum advertised for a shop manager, they wrote in their ad that they wanted "a gender and norm critical perspective." In other words, not even the checkout staff could be politically neutral.[14]

The Minister of Culture assured that the government had not commissioned the museum to work with norm criticism. She

12   http://www.svd.se/regeringen-forvandlar-museer-till-propagandacentraler/
     om/museidebatten.

13   http://www.svd.se/regeringen-forvandlar-museer-till-propagandacentraler/
     om/museidebatten.

14   http://www.svd.se/bah-kuhnkes-stravan-efter-mangfald-leder-till-enfald.

suggested that she and Ola Wong have lunch together and clear up the misunderstandings.

I thought it sounded pretty good when I read the answer, but Ola Wong didn't think so. He stated that the Minister of Culture cannot, of course, order a museum to engage in norm critical politics. That would be ministerial management which is forbidden in Sweden. On the other hand, the Ministry of Culture does control the issue via pronouncements that the museums then must interpret. They write regulation letters and policy documents. Above all, they govern by allocating money. Ola Wong's acidic comment: "The most obedient get candy."

According to a memorandum from the Ministry of Culture, the task of the State Historical Museums was to reflect contemporary Swedish identity and show that the country has also historically been multicultural. As it says: "A previous notion of an existing homogeneous nation has today been replaced by a society that strives instead to recognise and affirm its heterogeneity."[15]

The heads of the World Culture Museums and the National Historical Museums were allocated an extra four million, and the heads of the two agencies accompanied the Minister of Culture on a trip to Washington in September 2016. It's hard to believe that the three women didn't talk to each other about museum policy.

Ola Wong felt that the Minister of Culture was living in a parallel reality and gave several examples of the politicisation and disdain for knowledge that characterised the management of the World Culture Museums. He did not mince words. On norm criticism and post-colonialism, he wrote that "The problem is that they have become over-ideology, like an untouchable religion, and it is used as an excuse to cut away knowledge, heritage and institutional integrity." East Asia is a museum of Asian cultural history.

---

15   http://www.regeringen.se/contentassets/7491797b5ae64210915a38f078fb2091/
     en-museimyndighet-for-hela-den-historiska-utvecklingen-i-sverige-prome-
     moria-ku201601365kl.pdf.

The tabloid *Aftonbladet*'s cultural director reinforced that image. She noted that the cultural programme presented by the Green Party and the Minister of Culture had been rejected by everyone who read it. Yet it became government policy.

How did it go? On 19 March 2022, *Göteborgs-Posten* wrote that the World Culture Museum is best known for its recurring politically correct reminders.

## Everyone's Cultural Heritage

In May 2017, the Swedish National Heritage Board published its 240-page cultural heritage proposal *Vision for Cultural Heritage Work 2030*. They had been commissioned by the Government to develop a vision in 2014–16 and worked "in a broad dialogue" with 21 county administrative boards and several other stakeholders. Their findings were summarised thusly: "Everyone, regardless of background, feels that they can lay claim to the cultural heritage that has shaped Sweden." In plain language, this means a political frontal attack on the Swedish cultural heritage, which since the 17th century has had the sole task of celebrating and strengthening the nation, with its ethnically very homogeneous population. Naturally, I wonder how it is possible to make Iraqis, Afghans, and Syrians feel part of the Swedish cultural heritage, when they do not even feel like Swedes. In some cases, they even live in violence-generating hostility towards Sweden, like the stone-throwing and car-burning young Muslims who repeatedly riot and attack police and other blue-light personnel. Ola Wong is not merciful. Museums should not primarily spread knowledge about history and humanistic ideals:

> Instead, cultural environmental work should be an instrument to "unite people," "train empathy," create sustainable development and a sense of inclusion. Hallelujah! The government has decided that it is exclusionary and wrong to talk about yours and my cultural heritage. They are not even

allowed to try to delimit an "us," because then one can "forget to see and engage with the other."[16]

Ola Wong continued with his review of what is happening to Swedish museums. In September 2017, he wrote an article in *Svenska Dagbladet* in which he criticised the Minister of Culture for having given state museums a free hand to cull objects "as the icing on the cultural heritage cake."

This led to the sale of some museum objects. Customs received 1,170 SEK for a flag game. Other items, such as amulet rings and other finds from the Vendel and Viking periods, were thrown away because archaeologists did not want to create a market for ancient finds. If such a market existed, amateur excavators would go out and look for archaeological finds on historic sites.

Ola Wong said that the Minister of Culture preferred to use cultural heritage to shape tomorrow's society:

> A new influential group of archaeologists no longer digs in the ground at all but devotes itself to criticising other archaeologists (preferably safely dead) for various thought crimes. So digging for the truth about the past is not their goal.[17]

He also criticised the National Heritage Board's head of cultural heritage, Qaisar Mahmood, who thought he could discern murky motives and resistance to change among citizens who cherished the previously self-evident cultural heritage of rune stones, medieval churches, folk costumes and homestead gardens. He and the National Heritage Officer argued that cultural heritage was *exclusive*. In a column for the magazine *Fokus*, Qaisar Mahmood even compared some

---

16  https://www.svd.se/a/Ox13q/regeringen-anvander-museer-for-egna-politiska-mal.

17  https://www.svd.se/a/RkMLx/museichefer-utan-kunskap-forodande-for-kulturarvet.

protesting antiquarians at the National Heritage Board to Sweden Democrats.

*The Heritage Agenda* was heavily criticised by historians and archaeologists alike, but as the project was politically anchored at the highest level, this criticism did not matter. The Cultural Heritage Administration would continue to be an instrument for achieving the goals of integration policy.

## A Bold Idea for the Future

When it was decided in the mid-1970s that Sweden would be a multicultural country, it was not considered necessary to conduct an economic study. Decade after decade in the post-war period, labour immigration was a profitable business. In the early 1970s, immigrants contributed about 1% to GDP. It was then that Sweden, due to a recession, throttled labour immigration. Instead, so-called refugee immigration took over, and with it the cost-benefit picture changes.

Looking at the government's spring budget, published in mid-April 2017, the areas of *Migration* and *Gender Equality and the Settlement of Newly Arrived Immigrants* are set at 71.5 billion EUR for the year. Our budget then presented for the period 2016–2019 the figure 307 billion. This is a dramatic increase since autumn 2016 when the forecast for the same period was 169.6 billion. Note that this calculation does not include indirect costs of migration — mainly increased costs for schools and health care. To get an idea of the size, compare with the judicial system which, including the police, is budgeted at 179 billion. Defence is estimated to cost around 200 billion. That economist Tino Sanandaji doubts that the problems will be solved is not hard to understand:

> … the overall picture is disastrous and hardly suggests that integration challenges are transitory problems associated with initial asylum reception. There are few signs that the trend is reversing. The curve is pointing downwards, not upwards. It is also difficult to find evidence of dynamic

effects of hidden societal benefits of immigration, openness and diversity that have helped the economy to flourish.[18]

To this you could add extra costs for car and school fires, bombings and bomb threats against public buildings, death shootings, the costly Mafia trials, rapes, unlawful threats, pickpockets, shoplifting, home burglaries, throwing stones at police, fire brigades, ambulances, postmen, buses, destruction of police cars, fire engines, ambulances, lorries, increased insurance premiums, insurance fraud, reduced property values in immigrant areas, increased costs for private schools, etc.

I wonder why our entire Swedish elite has been so keen to cover up the cost of immigration. It is curious that the "refugee issue" has been given priority over concern for the country's own population. After all, it is the country's citizens who are not only the politicians' actual clients but also pay their salaries and the cost of the policies they pursue. Or, really, I don't wonder, at least not when it comes to politicians. If they fail to convince citizens that the multicultural society is economically viable — or at least worth the money — the project's legitimacy crumbles.

Since 2008, to this day, a book by the English economist and journalist Philipp Legrain, funded by the Globalisation Council and the Department for Education can be downloaded from the government's website. Legrain writes: "Establishment parties often offer boring, technocratic versions of the status quo. How about trying to inspire voters with a bold and clear idea of the future?"[19]

Sure, there are many examples in history of bold and clear ideas about the future. What about Lenin's or perhaps Stalin's visions for the Soviet Union, Hitler's of the millennial empire, Mao's culture

18   http://kvartal.se/artiklar/migration-och-vlfrdsstatens-finansiering.

19   Philipp Legrain, "Is Free Migration Compatible with a European-Style Welfare State?" Expert report no. 11. to Sweden's Globalisation Council. http://beta. regeringen.se/contentassets/880ac1658a944d31906ec26f9607c080/is-free-migrationcompatible-with-a-european-style-welfare-state

revolution, Khmer Rouge's rural society, and the Islamic State's Caliphate? I can't recall offhand a single society that has succeeded with "a bold and clear idea of the future." This is also true of Sweden's bold and clear idea of a multicultural society which, otherwise worryingly unmentioned, has produced a repression of opinion the likes of which we have never seen before in Sweden.

I wonder how many thousands of pounds Philipp Legrain made on this concoction of what he had previously written and been paid for by the EU.[20] This is how the government presentation still looks:

> Free immigration is often perceived as incompatible with a welfare state. This report analyses, using Sweden as an example, the extent to which rich welfare states attract migrants from poorer countries. The report shows that this view is too simplistic. Looking narrowly at the effects on state finances misses the broader economic benefits that actually help finance the welfare state. Migration should be seen as an opportunity — not a threat.[21]

Note the call for migration to be seen as an opportunity. Instead of giving a factual account of the costs, the government serves up propaganda. This is strange, as the government has previously stated that the socio-economic gains from labour migration stopped around 1985, since immigrants started exploiting the public welfare system to a much greater extent than before. Since then, there has been an annual deficit, i.e. excessive revenue that is transferred from the Swedish population to the immigrant population.

A decade later, the Ministry of Finance published the report *Immigration, Employment and Economic Impact* by Professor Jan Ekberg and Associate Professor Lars Andersson. The researchers noted that the immigration studies of the 1970s and 1980s never properly examined the economic effects of immigration. Even in such an important economic-policy document as the long-term

---

20  https://morklaggning.wordpress.com/2014/09/29/om-ideologisk-med-och-motvind-spraket-och-verkligheten/.

21  https://www.regeringen.se/rapporter/2008/05/underlagsrapport-11/.

studies, there was no in-depth examination of the economic effects of immigration.[22]

The report concludes that the likely costs for 1995 alone amounted to 20 billion SEK, which the researchers mean is a significant amount that could have been put to an alternative, i.e. better or more morally justifiable, use.

## Who Benefits from Disinformation?

One might have hoped that researchers would have put an end to the politicians' deception, but this was not the case. To add to the pile, Dick Harrison is one of Sweden's more well-known academic profiles. As a professor of history, he is both broad and deep in his knowledge. He is also a good stylist and often writes interesting articles in the daily press. He has argued that the mass immigration of our time to Sweden will probably prove profitable in the long run, because when you examine Swedish history, it has invariably been that way. Under the headline "Immigrants a gain for Sweden," he points to the United States as the prime example. He writes that there is not a single historical example of immigration being negative for the receiving country in the long run. On this point, our historical experience is crystal clear — the only form of immigration that has been, and is, directly harmful is that of warlike invasions.[23]

The claim raises the question: immigration for the benefit of whom? For the US, history is not about immigration, but about colonisation. The receiving and now almost extinct original population is a number of Indian tribes, both in North and South America. Surely, Dick Harrison cannot be suggesting that colonisation benefited them and their way of life?

Even if we accept the starting point that it is not about populations but about countries, the difficult question remains how Sweden

22  Ds 1995:68, p. 16.

23  https://www.svd.se/invandrarna-ar-en-vinst-for-sverige.

is to become a better country by mass importing and indefinitely supporting unemployed and poorly educated Eritreans, Somalis, Afghans, and Syrians. These are the groups that now dominate among those seeking and granted asylum in Sweden.

Dick Harrison has never accepted or changed his mind because of the criticism levelled at him. After his column on profitable immigration, published in the morning paper *Svenska Dagbladet* on New Year's Eve 2014, the objections were countless. In a follow-up article in the same paper, he defended himself by merely addressing those who had heaped invective on him, prompting economist Tino Sanandaji to conclude that the problem is not that Dick Harrison is uneducated about the history of immigration but that "the fellow seems fucking uneducable."

Who benefits from such disinformation? For scientists who celebrate truth-seeking, and perhaps even more so for journalists, it should be tempting to put a thumb in the eye of politicians who, for ideological reasons, mislead citizens. After all, it is a perfect way of legitimising their self-styled role as the fourth estate to their readerships. But it is only after the mass immigration of autumn 2015 that it became downright silly to claim that immigration was profitable. Surely no conversion has ever really taken place.

Instead of investigating mass immigration and controlling its consequences, instead of providing citizens and their voters with accurate data, politicians and their scientific and journalistic henchmen have belittled and concealed the problem. It is no exaggeration to state that all parliamentary parties except the Sweden Democrats have lied and deceived citizens on immigration issues. The boldest lie concerns profitability. Instead of telling citizens what immigration policy costs and what other pressing issues must wait, the politicians have worked hard to convince citizens that immigration is profitable.

## Pulling the Wool over People's Eyes

Peo Hansen is professor of political science at Linköping University. Politically, he is on the left and has, among other things, helped the Left Party with their migration policy programme. In 2021, he published the book *The Migration Myth*, the main thesis of which is that the unanimous experts who claimed that the reception of refugees in 2015 was an economic disaster were wrong. In 2015, then Finance Minister Magdalena Andersson said that Sweden would need to borrow lots of money to cope with the refugee crisis. Two years later, she stated in an interview that the state had not needed to borrow a single krona to finance the refugee reception and had even managed to pay off the national debt. The philosopher Roland Paulsen reviewed the book in *Dagens Nyheter* in the spring of 2022 and wrote:

> The years between the "refugee crisis" and the pandemic all meant surpluses for Sweden's public finances. Even at the municipal level, finances were good, Hansen shows. While municipal costs increased with the influx of refugees, so did government subsidies, whose stimulus eventually led to increased tax revenues. In 2016, only nine of Sweden's 290 municipalities reported a deficit. The Swedish Association of Local Authorities and Regions described it as a historic result, one of the "strongest ever."[24]

Peo Hansen's explanation is that the state does not function in the same way as a household, which must balance expenditure and income. Since the state has a monopoly on money, it can always create more through the Bank of Sweden, or by simply raising spending. So, when the state spent money to cope with the refugee crisis, it provided a stimulus to the economy.

Now, this view is not exactly unknown, either among politicians or economists. It's known as helicopter money, after an argument made in the 1960s by economist and Nobel Prize winner Milton

---

24  https://www.dn.se/kultur/roland-paulsen-i-dag-vet-alla-att-flyktingarna-inte-innebar-en-systemkollaps/.

Friedman about a hypothetical helicopter dropping cash from the sky. In the short term, it may boost consumption and thus the economy, but in the long term it risks destroying the basic incentives for work and enterprise that are crucial to driving an economy. It's like peeing yourself when you're cold. At first, it's warm and nice, but then…

Anyway, what matters according to Peo Hansson is not the money but the work that is done — and immigrants do very important work in Sweden. Almost 30% of those working in elderly care are foreign-born and for cleaners the figure is 60%. As many as 51% of all bus and tram drivers, 49% of all taxi drivers, and 42% of all restaurant workers are born in another country. If we add those citizens with foreign-born parents, the percentages rise further. All of these can be considered "income," unlike, for example, all the journalists, economists and politicians who, in socio-economic terms, are "costs."

This can be seen as the third major attempt to pull wool over the eyes of those who claim that immigration is a juicy minus item in the state budget.[25] The first attempt was a report by the auditing firm PWC in 2014, commissioned by the municipality of the town Sandviken, in the north of Sweden. It claimed that the municipality earned over half a billion a year from its foreign-born residents. On average, this amounts to more than 145,000 SEK per person per year. *Dagens Nyheter* published the news widely and uncritically, because it was in line with their wishful thinking. They asked the auditing firm PWC whether Sandviken was a special case and got the answer that Sweden could not manage economically without immigration. One of the "proofs" highlighted was that Finland was doing badly. Presumably their immigration was too low.[26]

The clients got the result they wanted. This was done by counting the two-year government grant as profit and excluding all costs,

25   https://uvell.se/2021/04/01/900-miljarder-del-2/.

26   https://www.dn.se/nyheter/sverige/tjanar-over-en-halv-miljard-pa-invandrin-gen/.

about 70%, paid by the state and county councils. Things did not get any better once it became clear that the Sandviken report had mainly calculated the immigrants' own income, not the benefits accrued to the municipality. The calculation example appears to be an almost desperate attempt to convince the Swedish people of the profitability of immigration.

After a while, the politicians' lies were discovered, but even before then the Sandviken report had spread like wildfire across the Internet. Some 18,000 people liked it on Facebook and two members of the government applauded. Apparently, they couldn't count. Perhaps most outrageously, *Dagens Nyheter* refused to publish a correction, arguing that it was not they who had done or commissioned the survey, and thus they were not responsible.

Five years later, Sandviken had a budget deficit of 67 million. The main reason was that they no longer had any state reimbursements to cover the extra costs that immigrants brought with them. In the Confederation of Swedish Enterprise's business ranking — a list of places in Sweden where it is best to start and run a business — Sandviken was ranked 244 out of 290.[27]

The second attempt was the 2015 report by trade union economists Sandro Scocco and Lars Fredrik Andersson, which showed that refugee immigration had contributed 900 billion in revenue for Sweden. *Dagens Nyheter* reported as uncritically as before:

Immigration has been good business for Sweden. Without the post-war influx of foreign-born taxpayers, the tax coffers would be missing an average of 65 billion a year. We would not have been able to afford as much in the way of roads, railways, research or defence. [...] That immigration would still be profitable — despite the high unemployment of many recent immigrant groups and their heavy dependence on municipal welfare — Scocco and Andersson base their argument on the fact that the 1.6 million-strong group of foreign-born has fewer elderly people with

27   https://www.expressen.se/nyheter/sandvikens-miljonforlust-fem-ar-efter-vinstrapporten/.

high costs and more people of working age than the native-born group. Therefore, despite their lower employment rate, the foreign-born are able to finance society's costs for their own group's consumption of social services and transfers.[28]

Economist Tino Sanandaji called the report lousy research, in part because it used the researchers' own made-up revenue figures instead of real statistics from SCB or the Swedish Tax Agency.[29]

## Almost Bankrupt

What Peo Hansen does not explain is that the state subsidies that boosted the economy were taken as loans and came from other areas. They were temporary and as soon as they disappeared, the municipalities had to take the hit. Eventually, new arrivals had to stand on their own two feet, work and pay taxes. If they pay significantly less tax on average than the local population, there will be a cost in the end. Several municipalities ended up on the brink of ruin because of the cost of refugees. Filipstad was the most high-profile case in the media. The municipality almost went bankrupt because on the labour market there was no demand for foreign-born illiterates.

No matter how you massage the economy, it can never be profitable when an ever-shrinking native working population must provide for an ever expanding foreign one — one that also consumes plenty of welfare.

In 2018, economist Joakim Ruist showed that an average asylum migrant has a lifetime cost of between 1.7–3 million SEK. In total, refugees cost around 41 billion SEK per year, or about 1% of GDP.[30] However, the real cost is much higher, as neither subsidised employment nor the costs of direct reception are included.

---

28  https://www.dn.se/ekonomi/invandringens-vinst-900-miljarder/.

29  https://tino.us/2015/07/arenarapporten-varfor-anvanda-riktig-statistik-pa-skatteintakter-nar-vi-kan-anta-fram-vinst/.

30  https://www.svd.se/a/wEmGdL/tre-miljoner-kronor-per-flykting.

Only a third of all migrants from the Middle East/North Africa ever reach a level of self-sufficiency for the OECD poverty line (12,600 SEK per month), and that includes all the jobs created by the state and local authorities that contribute to "employment." For foreign-born people, it takes 13–14 years to reach this low level of self-sufficiency.

What is not very visible in these calculations are all the "extra" costs of immigration. In her *Handbook for Cheats* (2021), *Dagens Nyheter*'s editorial writer Hanne Kjöller writes that those who, for various reasons, apply for benefits to support themselves and are granted them are usually not checked. When they do, cheating is often revealed.

This subsidy leakage is well known. There are thousands of pages where experts and investigators both go through the material. There are government reports, consultation responses and letters, but nothing happens. This is the crux of the matter when it comes to the Swedish welfare state. It has grown into a gigantic, entirely tax-funded, organisational system, a "Welfare Industrial Complex" consisting of various interacting components:

- The Swedish Migration Board, the National Board of Health and Welfare and the municipal social administrations.

- The clients, i.e. the recipients of income support, unemployment benefits, disabled people who receive disability assistance and so on.

- Many companies involved in the production of welfare with state funding.[31]

Despite their differences, all these actors have a common goal, namely, to maximise politicians' allocations to the overall welfare, i.e. to themselves. Together they form a finely calibrated machine of

---

31  https://detgodasamhallet.com/2022/03/31/patrik-engellau-incitamenten/.

intertwined interests. Nobody may like illegal disabled imports from Somalia, but nobody has anything against legal disabled imports from Somalia either. It is the supply of clients that ultimately makes the system grow. Everyone sees their own benefits in maximising the turnover of the system.

It's not a question of small change. In March 2022, "The commission for Tax Benefit" writes

> Every year, 18 billion SEK is paid out incorrectly from the state welfare systems. It ranges from the occasional mistake to serious organised crime. Despite several government inquiries proposing both new legislation and organisational changes, the problems persist.[32]

## The Welfare Industrial Complex

During the 1970s, the number of public employees increases from half a million to three times that number in Sweden. Part-time elected politicians were replaced by paid professional politicians, and we had a municipal bureaucracy that was responsible for the practice of welfare. The country's small, insignificant municipal offices were replaced by gigantic administrative buildings.

The Social Democrats wanted to implement what they still in their party programme call "a general welfare model." "The strong society" is another key concept, meaning a society in which social policy was extended to include everyone.

The strong society should, in its turn, be interpreted as more power for politicians and authorities — a power that is not financed by production but by rapid and extremely large tax increases. It became a bit like the cartoon where the owner cuts off the dog's tail to get something to feed him with. A strong society needs professional politicians and many helpers. The result we see today, in the form of a welfare industry.

---

32    https://skattenytta.se/ovrigt/brott-mot-valfardssystemen/.

The guiding principle of the welfare society is justice, a reliable vote magnet. Wealth is unfair if there are those who are poorer. Welfare policy therefore becomes an instrument for levelling out inequalities. Here is the embryo of a senseless political idea, namely that the state's task is to compensate the weak for their disadvantage. It is senseless because the state turns a blind eye to the cause of the disadvantage.

A contrived but at least for me telling example is about a pair of twins. One of the brothers invests in studies and a vocational training. He refrains from a fun youth life and turns his nose up at books that he himself finds boring. Then he graduates and gets a job. Not a top job, but a rather boring one. But he supports himself and is no trouble to anyone. The other brother burns his candle at both ends and actually has a very enjoyable life. Lots of fun nights and days, lots of sex and lots of drugs, but no education and burnt out at forty. For him, it's time to put his future in the hands of the state. It's not fun but the consequence of him having a lot of fun. He becomes a welfare recipient, which means that the state takes from the income of the hard-working and profitable brother and gives to the unresponsive brother, so that he can live at roughly the same standard.

It is an injustice when self-inflicted weakness is rewarded. The social security supported man is hardly grateful to his working brother, for he does not understand the connection. Nor is he grateful to the state that provides for him, because he believes he is in a position where he has a right to demand subsidy funding. In other words, the state rewards weakness, which is a bad and unfair political idea.

Our contemporary version of the welfare society has done away with the cautionary tale. Just because you're living the flea life doesn't mean you end up in hell. Life could be acceptable even if you don't get an education and eventually lose your job. You don't have to end up on the street, even if you are abandoned, and even though you have small children. It doesn't have to go to hell just because you've managed to get to Sweden and yet you've neither learned the

language nor have any skills that could lead to a job and self-sufficiency. If you can prove to society in one way or another that you are
at a disadvantage, that you are a victim, then you are entitled to the
support of society. The priority of justice leads to a society where the
state steals most of the money earned by citizens through work, to
distribute to the "more needy."

A strong state is a problematic goal because it leads to weak citizens. Moreover, a state that first seizes most of the people's income
through taxation and then distributes it according to a Robin Hood
model (take from the rich and give to the poor) makes citizens into
subjects. In the long run: calculating, manipulative and, towards the
state, demanding citizens. Those who appear to be the most dissatisfied, the most unfairly treated, have the greatest chance of having
their demands met.

The political opponents do not protest. Welfare is an unequivo-
cally positive thing. All politicians, from right to left, like it.

The so-called tax ratio in 1960 was 29%, below the average for
OECD countries. After that, taxes skyrocketed and Sweden ended up
in a top five position among all the countries in the world, a position
it still has.

In 1976, the world-famous author Astrid Lindgren wrote a satirical tale, *Pomperipossa*. She had discovered that she was paying 102%
of her income in taxes. The Social Democrats lost the election, probably in part because Astrid Lindgren had drawn the attention of the
Swedish people to unreasonable marginal taxes. However, the Centre
Party coalition were not quick to cut taxes when they came to power.
The welfare industry still needed to be financed.

Anyone who does not fall for the rhetoric celebrating welfare and
starts asking critical questions about welfare will discover more problems. Welfare is a contract between the state and the individual citizen. Of course, single mothers, for example, should be able to claim
social support, not least with reference to their children. Welfare society gets plenty of single mothers. Men do not have to shoulder the

responsibility of being the breadwinner and women do not have to be particularly discriminating in their choice of partner. Not so long ago, it was a disaster for an unmarried woman to become pregnant. That is no longer the case.

The Social Democrats never knew how to stop their reforms, and we see the results. They created a society of weak, obedient, and demanding but also dissatisfied citizens. This raises the question of whether a welfare society can be stable at all. Does it perhaps harbour the seeds of its own demise? As we know, not all societies are stable.

I have saved the most problematic findings for last. When the exploitation of citizens reaches its peak, when the state can no longer squeeze more money out of the working population, then the only thing left to do is to cut welfare. Fewer police officers, fewer ambulances, fewer rescue helicopters, less social assistance, less health care, fewer pensions, etc. What remains is a high-tax society with a heavy burden of dependency. And consequently: declining welfare. The incentive for the well-educated and profitable to seek another country is growing stronger. A country where they can arrange a better future for themselves and their children. In other words, white flight. The best simply pack their bags and leave. What remains is the weak population, whose interests have been prioritised by welfare policy. A poor, demanding and dissatisfied population.

## A Decent Social Contract

Let us conclude this chapter with a rather telling excerpt from a text written by "Anders," who calls himself "an ordinary family man."[33] Both he and his wife have been studying for many years while on small incomes in the hopes of finding interesting and well-paid jobs. He is outraged, not to say despairing, that the wealth that hardworking Swedes have created for themselves is being squandered. If the abuse does not stop, he sees himself forced to emigrate with his

---

33  https://morklaggning.wordpress.com/2015/11/29/sonderfallet/.

family to a country that, unlike Sweden, can offer a decent social contract and hope for a secure future:

> Swedish politics and the media have become corrupted. Politicians do not
> understand that they are supposed to work for the good of the citizens,
> and the media do not understand that they are supposed to protect the
> public's interests against these politicians. Instead, politicians seem to have
> got the preposterous idea of outbidding each other in giving away the
> common property of citizens to people from other countries. It is as if the
> manager of the bank were to empty our accounts and hand out the money
> because she thought it felt so good to help. But my money is not the bank's
> to do with as it pleases. The government turns over large sums of money
> that should go to our old people's pensions, our children's schooling, and
> our care and security if we get sick. It's what we've paid the world's highest
> taxes for, and it's a shameful betrayal of the voters to squander it on things
> we didn't agree on. It's very easy to be generous with other people's money,
> but that's exactly what politicians shouldn't be. They have a special trust to
> manage in a welfare and high-tax society, but have generally abused that
> trust for decades. The only reason they have not been caught is that, in
> symbiosis with journalists, they have hidden their deception in every con-
> ceivable way. [...]

I don't want to pay more to a society that gives me and my family less
and less back but gives more and more money to more and more people from other parts of the world. People who often come here on false
grounds and with false identities, who often avoid paying taxes themselves
through shady deals, and who send billions of Swedish kronor every year
to relatives in their home countries, instead of using them on the Swedish
market. It is beyond me how Swedish politicians could forget their responsibility to their own citizens and voters, and furthermore fail to understand that they are driving away those who form the basis of the relative
prosperity to which they now think the whole world should have access.
Apparently they do not understand multiplication and division either, or
they would have realised long ago that our prosperity is vanishing if it is
used unwisely or distributed to too many people. Along the way, they have
imported values and a violent ideology that I would not wish on my worst
enemies, and to which I certainly do not intend to expose my children and
grandchildren.

# Law and Politics

## The Party Is Always Right

DEMOCRACIES ARE expected to establish a clear dividing line between politics and law, with the judicial function of the legal system taking precedence over politics. Everyone knows that this is very important, because we see how it can go in countries where politicians control the courts. The best-known example is probably the Soviet Union with the infamous Moscow trials of 1936–38. Most of the old leaders of the Bolshevik Party were convicted in show trials and executed.

Sweden, which is usually classed as one of the world's strongest democracies, does not have a legal system that is free from politics, except in one very important respect. Politicians cannot control the judgments that are handed down. I do not believe that Swedish courts are corrupt, but Sweden has a kind of light variant of the East German order: *the party is always right.*

The courts' judgments should be understood as interpretations of politicians' instructions. Their legal proceedings, alongside practice, are the most important source of law.

In post-war Sweden, there has been a consensus on the supremacy of politics over the law. The welfare state has symbolised justice — not the law. This is a socialist approach, in stark contrast to the

Anglo-Saxon liberal tradition, where the law protects the individual against the state.[1]

A clear example of how Swedish politicians can override the lawyers was given by the so-called Upper Secondary School Act. In 2015, over 163,000 people sought asylum in Sweden. Of these, 35,369 were registered as children. After a very long wait, about 9,000 had their applications rejected, after having their age assessed by the Migration Agency.

These were not children but young men. Women were virtually absent. Almost all of them were Afghans and belonged to the Hazar ethnic group. These "unaccompanied children" were neither unaccompanied nor children, and many had never even lived in Afghanistan but came from Iran or Syria. They all lacked valid identification documents because the possibility of obtaining asylum was improved if they could not present a valid passport.

The Upper Secondary School Act gave young men who had been refused asylum but had been waiting for a decision for more than 15 months, the possibility of being granted asylum if they registered as students within three months. In addition, they had to have managed to find a job within six months of completing their education. This was completely absurd, as virtually nobody had the prior knowledge or language skills needed to complete such studies. It was not difficult to figure out that there was also a considerable risk that they would disrupt the classes in which they were placed. The bill came from the government, facilitated both by members of the Social Democrats and the environmentalist party.

The Legislative Council gave the thumbs down. They considered that the proposal did not meet the requirements for the preparation of legislation. The new rules could be questioned in principle and the consequences were very difficult to foresee. They referred to the fact that the migration courts had also criticised the proposal and wrote:

---

1    https://journals.lub.lu.se/st/article/view/8645/7782.

The Legislative Council shares this assessment, and considers that the limit has been reached here for what is acceptable in terms of how legislation can be drafted. [...] The possibilities for a residence permit do not depend on the individual's circumstances, but on the actions of the Migration Agency. It is highly questionable whether this is an objectively acceptable principle. [...] In Swedish law, too, it is not a principle to allow lengthy processing times in themselves to be grounds for granting applications of various kinds. In this respect, the proposal raises questions that have not been analysed at all in the Legislative Advice Document.[2]

The senior lawyers also questioned whether the intention to study was sufficient to obtain a residence permit. It was not required that studies would actually be pursued — there wouldn't even be any verification that the studies had begun.

The proposal was tabled in Parliament by the Left Party, the Green Party, and the Social Democrats. To get it through, it needed the support of one more party, and that was the Centre Party. Annie Lööf, the leader of the Centre Party, who is a lawyer by training, said that al-though the bill was ill-conceived and poorly drafted, the humanitarian consequences would be too great if it were stopped:

The Centre Party's line has consistently been that unaccompanied minors who were minors when they arrived and who have suffered from the Migration Agency's long processing times should be given a second chance. Our overall assessment is therefore still that we will let this law pass. These young people will now have three months to apply for a new individual assessment based on the new law.[3]

According to the government, the Upper Secondary School Act would cost just under 3 billion SEK. But a calculation by the

2   https://www.riksdagen.se/sv/dokument-lagar/dokument/motion/sverige-behover-en-forfattningsdomstol_H6021022.

3   https://www.centerpartiet.se/press/pressmeddelande/nyhetsarkiv-2018/2018-04-24-annie-loof-darfor-slapper-centerpartiet-igenom-lagen-om-ensamkommande.

Parliamentary Investigation Service shows that the cost up to 2020 has been exceeded by between 1.4-1.9 billion SEK.[4]

One of the consequences was a wave of robberies and sexual assaults in Uppsala. Around 80% of the crimes were committed by unaccompanied minors, now known as 'young people.' The morning paper *Svenska Dagbladet* reports:

> The situation is similar in central Gothenburg and Stockholm. Moroccan street children and Afghan unaccompanied minors are a growing concern for the police. Many are taken into custody or arrested daily but are released immediately because of their age. The risk of recidivism seems to be the rule rather than the exception, which should make prosecutors rethink their approach. Police officers I have spoken to describe it as a Sisyphean task to be forced to arrest and release the same people, with no consequences for the criminal.[5]

In 2021, figures from the Migration Agency showed that 171 of the 7,763 minors were granted asylum. It was also reported that the Migration Agency was working on "voluntary return," but no Afghan national who was to be deported had returned home. Nor had the police carried out any deportations to Afghanistan since the Taliban took over. In theory, therefore, people can be deported to Afghanistan, but in practice this did not happen. With the secondary school reform, it became clear how weak the legal advice was. Politicians were able to ignore the harsh and justified criticism of the lawyers.

## Law Is Politics in Disguise

The Bar Association organises two "buddy networks" for lawyers, *Hilda* and *Ruben*. They help steer important political decisions. Those

---

4    https://www.dn.se/nyheter/sverige/moderaterna-gymnasielagen-har-blivit-for-dyr/.

5    https://www.svd.se/a/9a8pM/gatubarn-bakom-ranvag-i-uppsala.

who do not belong to these networks have limited chances of making a career — the risk of being fired is greater. They connect not only lawyers, but also judges, prosecutors, the chief of the National Police and other senior police officers, the head of the Customs Service, and the head of the Migration Board. There is also the Chancellor of Justice. In particular, these networks have attracted Social Democrats. Cecilia Renfors is a member of the Hilda network and gives the following motivation:

> Nowadays, there are very many women in managerial and other senior roles in the judiciary, but it still seems to be a bigger and more difficult step for many women than for men to apply for managerial or other more qualified jobs. The work Hilda is doing to bridge such difficulties and close the gap is important. A network focusing on these issues is still needed.[6]

That sounds good, for those who believe that gender equality is one of the most important issues in law. In 2011, the morning paper *Skånska Dagbladet* was more critical and wrote under the headline "Networks that threaten legal certainty":

> Today, seven out of nine members of the Judicial Board, which appoints most of the country's judges, belong to one of the feminist networks Hilda, Ida or Ruben. Only the two representatives of the public, two MPs from the Social Democrats and the Moderates, are independent and hopefully autonomous. And the claims to power do not stop at formal decision making. One journalist, who drew attention to the Auditor General's criticism of the composition of the Judicial Board in a number of articles, experienced unpleasant accusations and pressure. It is safe to assume that the same approach has been used in other contexts, probably with success.[7]

In the spring of 2021, lawyer and economist Magnus Stenlund delivered even harsher criticism. When he studied law in the 1980s, it was a given that the judiciary would strive for impeachable integrity. They

---

6   https://advokatakademien.advokatsamfundet.se/hilda/om-hilda/Hildas-medlemmar/cecilia-renfors/.

7   https://www.flashback.org/t2783489.

did not comment on political views. It was directly inappropriate to
have such opinions, as they risked compromising the objectivity of
the judiciary. As a lawyer, and even as a judge, to be part of political
networks such as *Hilda*, *Ruben* or *Legally Lady* — with strong views
on immigration, climate change, LGBTQ issues and feminism on the
agenda, among other things — would have been unthinkable. Magnus
Stenlund notes that the Social Democrats have notoriously exploited
the power of patronage and filled the judiciary with party affiliated
lawyers, and he thinks he sees the end of the country's time as a constitutional state.

He says that Cecilia Renfors and he were studying law at the
same time and writes that at the time she was "a little grey mouse"
who didn't make much of a fuss. That is no longer the case. Cecilia
Renfors's political correctness, membership in the Social Democratic
Party and being of the weaker and allegedly discriminated gender
have given her a spick and span career. In December 2018, Cecilia
Renfors was appointed a member of the Supreme Court, which is as
far as a lawyer can go in Sweden. She took office in September 2019.
Magnus Stenlund writes:

> The new Supreme Court judge Cecilia Renfors, with great potential to
> become the most dangerous person in power for Sweden in the coming
> decade, is an excellent example of how it works. She has been a political
> activist, feminist and multicultural activist for virtually her entire career.
> As practically unsackable, in the Supreme Court she will be able to con-
> tinue engaging in left-wing activism, ranging from imposing the Global
> Compact and other upcoming EU and UN agendas with court precedent,
> to giving Islamophobia the broad meaning she argued for as judicial
> ombudsman. Her involvement in the Legislative Council also allows her
> to play a dual role, helping to bring about deeply problematic laws, such
> as the Upper Secondary School Act, and then establishing their legality
> through rulings in the Supreme Court.[8]

8    https://www.friatider.se/rattsvasendet-har-blivit-en-lekstuga-aktivister-och-
     kriminella.

## Displeased Voices

There is one public platform where it is still possible not only to have an important political debate, but also to criticise all kinds of contemporary madness: the Internet. But even there the noose is tightening. A couple of years ago, the Swedish TV channel *SwebbTV* was thrown off YouTube. Note that it wasn't just distasteful material that was deleted. SwebbTV's entire catalogue of several hundred items was removed. So, it wasn't a crackdown on individual items, it was a rapidly growing alternative TV channel being silenced on YouTube. Swedish authorities were of course happy to be rid of a displeasing voice. YouTube could have responded by shutting down what they regard as hate speech, but they didn't; they went along with the Swedish government. That makes it legitimate to use the term censorship. No transparency was admitted and YouTube did not feel the need to justify their decision.

Nor does YouTube inform broadcasters that their programmes will be deleted. They just disappear. Much the same thing happened with the journalistic channel *Investigation Sweden* (Sw. *Granskning Sverige*), which was shut down after pressure from the media giant Bonniers. Jeanette Gustafsdotter, who was to become the social democratic minister for culture and democracy was overjoyed:

> Google has listened to the criticism of Swedish media houses and has taken its responsibility. The goal is to shut down all accounts that do illegal material. It will be a form of self-regulation instead of legislation. But this is the best way to deal with illegality.[9]

Self-regulation? Irregularities? What *Granskning Sverige* did was to call up journalists and put them up against the wall. Then they posted these calls on YouTube. It's unfair: pulling down the pants of journalists, you can't do that! The tabloid *Expressen* claimed that this was

9 https://www.expressen.se/news/google-stanger-ner-reviewing-sweden's-head-account-pa-youtube/.

neither about freedom of expression nor was it any kind of citizen journalism but "harassment of professionals who support society."

For the general election in September 2022, Google appointed a new censorship department headed by 42-year-old Sara Övreby, labelled as a socio-political director. Her mission was said to be "bridging the gap between technology and politics." She explained: "Now that many people are turning to Google and YouTube to find information about the elections, it is especially important that our platforms are not misused." She has also said that most of the censored material is removed even before it was posted on YouTube.

In the future, Google will intensify its cooperation with both the Swedish Civil Contingencies Agency and the Swedish Psychological Defence Agency. It is not surprising that the major network operators are keen to please the Swedish authorities. It was taxpayers' money that was used when they gave Facebook's server halls in the town Luleå an establishment subsidy of 140 million SEK.

## Lex Åberg

In 1941, the notorious antisemite Einar Åberg bought a bookshop in central Stockholm. In the same year, he founded the "Anti-Jewish Fighting League of Sweden" with the aim of "the total annihilation of Judaism in Sweden." In the window of the bookshop, he put up a sign that read "Jews and half-Jews are not allowed." There was often trouble in the shop and Einar Åberg was prosecuted and convicted for disorderly conduct. This did not stop him from continuing to put up new signs in his bookshop. When he also began to distribute leaflets internationally, pressure came from Jewish organisations in the United States and a new provision was enacted, "hate speech" (HMF). At first it was called the Lex Åberg, because Einar Åberg was the first person to be convicted in 1948.

The HMF was founded with direct reference to a specific ethnic group, the Jews. It is this that makes the first wording include both descent and creed as definitions of an ethnic group. Some Jews see themselves as a people, others stress that it is not ethnicity but religion that holds Jews together. The more general context is that members of the ethnic group that is in the majority and in power in a country should not be able to oppress members of other ethnic groups. I think neither lawyers nor politicians could have imagined the journey that this section of the law would take after it was passed by the Swedish Parliament.

## What Is Incitement?

During the 1960s, racism became the focus of Swedish social debate. It was not very relevant for Sweden, which was still ethnically very homogeneous, but what happened in the US and South Africa in particular became important issues for a politically radicalised generation of students. Fighting apartheid in South Africa also became an issue close to the hearts of Swedish Social Democrats and Liberals. Now the law came to include "race, colour, national or ethnic origin, or creed." As the concept of "incitement" was also given an increasingly broad definition, the provision of the law was on a collision course with freedom of expression.

One of those who saw the danger most clearly was the liberal and former editor-in-chief of *Dagens Nyheter*, Svante Nycander, who wrote in a memorial for a friend:

> Since 1948, hate speech has been given a broader meaning by both legislation and judicial practice. Initially, it was a matter of threats, slander or defamation against a group of the population with a particular creed. Mainly in response to the UN Convention against Racial Discrimination, Parliament adopted several amendments in 1970. It was then required that the criminal act had to be in the nature of a threat or an expression of contempt and that it was directed against a group by reference to race, colour, national or ethnic origin or creed.

Contempt is a broader concept than defamation and libel. According to the preamble to the 1970 legislation, it is not necessary to single out certain races or ethnic groups. The provision can be applied if, for example, a certain race is praised in such a way that all other races can be considered defamed.[10]

As Svante Nycander writes, when Sweden signed the UN Convention on Racial Discrimination, the criteria of *defamation* and *libel* were replaced with the difficult-to-interpret criterion of *disrespect*. The intention was to broaden the scope of the provision to include ridicule. The next extension came in 1982, when the text of the law referred not only to ethnic groups but also to "other such groups of persons."

As a synonym for "expresses disrespect," "expresses itself in a derogatory manner" and the term "defamatory" are also used. "Spread" is also a crucial term. If you write private notes, you can write whatever you want without being judged. But if you post them on Facebook or Flashback, for example, they are considered to have been 'disseminated.'

Hate has two meanings. One is an exhortation, like "Hey, now you/we have to scalp all Moldovans!" In other words, it is an invitation to physically and/or psychologically harm the persons against whom the acts are directed. The second meaning is 'to incite in the sense of terrorising.'

The verb 'to incite' refers to a psychological attack that is intended to make the person or persons being incited do something that they do not really want to do. It is not only people who are incited. Wikipedia writes:

Incitement is a form of hunting a prey animal. The term has come to be used in two different senses: wild animals hunting prey in packs. People who hunt wildlife in such a way as to incite them.[11]

10   https://morklaggning.wordpress.com/2021/04/06/hets-mot-folkgrupp/.

11   https://sv.wikipedia.org/wiki/Hetsjakt.

Those who are outside the course of events, as a court always is, should have little difficulty in determining what constitutes a threat or incitement, since both concepts can be linked to acts and courses of events that are likely to lead primarily to physical harm.

This does not apply to terms such as 'defamatory' and 'derogatory' along with their various synonyms. The latter are about how one experiences or feels what is said. If I say "Hello, nigga" to a black man, he is likely to feel slighted. But if his black friend says it, it is more likely to be perceived as a joint affirmation of identity. In other words, it is both experience and context that determine how the concept is interpreted.

Take this to a court. To make a judgement, one must make a distinction between people — even a racial distinction — in this way of reasoning. A white man may not say the same things as a black man to another black man. In the one case it is prosecutable, in the other it is not. That kind of legislation, or perhaps rather interpretation of the law, because it is the interpretation that is slipping, has no place in the administration of justice.

It is easy to give more examples, but I think this one is quite sufficient — especially since we already have a functioning legislation on *defamation and aggravated defamation* where — unlike the crime of *hatred against the people* — it is the person who is defamed who has to report to the police in order for a prosecution to be initiated. This makes it impossible for politicians and other outsiders to turn a blind eye.

In the case of this legislation, prosecution can be initiated by the public prosecutor without any victim having made a complaint. This is the practice — the ethnic group being targeted is irrelevant. In the case of press offences against freedom or freedom of expression, it is the Chancellor of Justice, who has the government as his client, who brings the charges. It happens very rarely, but when it does, it is almost impossible to stop. The Chancellor of Justice makes the laws. In other words, with the interpretation and handling of "hatred of the people," the table has been set for political prosecution.

In 2002, "sexual orientation" was added, and in 2019 so was "transgender identity or expression." Today, "hatred against a group of people" is a crime which, according to Chapter 16 of the Criminal Code, makes it illegal to express disdain for a *group of people or other such group of persons with reference to race, colour, national or ethnic origin, creed or sexual orientation."*

In 2014, a man was charged with incitement to hatred after he wrote on Facebook that "it's not normal to wake up to the sound of donkey with a stomach ache." He posted the comment on Facebook, along with a film of the Muslim service.

Is this incitement? Is it a threat? No! Is it derogatory? Yes, but so what? Since it is directed at Muslims, are Muslims a minority? The answer is no. Islam is the world's second largest religion, and its practitioners are by no means a minority, least of all a people, i.e. an ethnic minority.

The prosecutor defended himself: "Taken out of context, the comment appears inoffensive. But together with the video and the fact that it got a huge distribution, it is not criticism of religion but pure mockery."

However, threats and mockery are not at all identical. And for the prosecution it is completely irrelevant whether the mockery was widely disseminated. There are no gradations here; law is about either/or. Either a statement has been widely disseminated or it has not. Either a defendant is guilty, or he or she is innocent. The court does not sentence a person to, say, "76% guilty," which may well be the case. If two people come into conflict with each other, they can both be guilty. But that is not the way a court works. And for contagion, either it has taken place, or it has not. As it was, the "donkey man" was acquitted. Today, two decades later, the "donkey man" would probably have been convicted.

When his prosecution was challenged, the prosecutor explained that the taunt had to be qualified as a threat because the police had to be called out to protect the man from angry people who had read the comment. This means that the offence should not be considered minor either.

But it is the man prosecuted who is being threatened — not just linguistically but physically, by people who clearly don't give a damn about freedom of speech. However politically attractive it may seem, it is important not to judge backwards. A lynch mob attacking a man who has spoken contemptuously about Islamic prayer calls is something other than mob violence and very dangerous, not only for the person being attacked but also for the society in which it takes place.

The judiciary does not need this broad interpretation of what constitutes incitement at all. It is the politicians who need it, which leads to the question of whether citizens need it. The answer is no, because it is used as a restriction on the freedom of expression to which Swedish citizens are entitled under the Constitution.

## What Is an Ethnic Group?

A further problematic slippage in relation to this legislation is the interpretation of the concept of ethnic group.

In Norway, the Swedes are an ethnic group because the majority are Norwegians and the Swedes are a minority. The term ethnic group is not usually used to refer to the majority population. The term 'people' fits better — confirming that the practice of the word 'ethnic group' is that its members are in some form of minority. Swedes in the US are also a people, but there is no majority, at least not in the form of an ethnically defined group. Thus, those with white, blue, yellow or black skin are not ethnic groups. Neither are gays or trannies, any more than one-armed window cleaners.

The ambiguity that exists with the concept of ethnic group is primarily about which individuals should be included in the group.

Membership is biological — who your parents are determines membership. Acceptance can also be legally or socially defined.

In the description of the crime of hatred against a group of people, there is a clarification that *says "...or other* such group of *persons with reference to race, colour, national or ethnic origin, creed or sexual orientation."*

Are these groups? In the social science literature, *ethnicity* is a very well-defined concept, and this is broadly true of the group concept as well. Group members know, are familiar with, or at least recognise each other. The legal definition is simply wrong and weakens citizens' constitutional freedom of expression.

Of the listed specifications, only *ethnic origin* is relevant. Where ethnicity and nationality are in practice the same (one country, one people), *national* is also applicable, but for the other listed definitions it is in fact wrong to consider them as groups. They are *categories*, not *groups*. This neglect of the distinction between groups and categories is of great importance, both politically and legally.

What distinguishes a category from a group is that those grouped together in a category do not know or know of each other. To put it more bluntly, since they do not exist on their own terms, they cannot be victims of crime as a collective.

One objection could be that the judiciary is sovereign in deciding what meaning a court should attach to various concepts. After all, they have indicated here which categories they want to add to the concept of ethnic group. A comparable example is how rape is interpreted in the Swedish legal system. A person who, against a woman's will, fingers her sex and inserts a finger between her labia can be convicted of rape. That this is a sexual assault is clear, but it is not rape as it is understood in common language. Why should the judiciary stick with its own and divergent definitions of the offence? It is completely unnecessary because the punishment is the central issue. There is no reason to abandon descriptions of offences that correspond to common language. A spade should be called a spade.

For example, one of the terms that has led to a prosecution and conviction for hate speech is *"blatte."* *Blatte* is a slang word for immigrant in the same way as *svenne* is for Swede. If it's OK to say *svenne*, why should *blatte* be criminalised? If there is one institution that must never lose touch with living reality, it is the judicial system.

The citizens convicted of "hate speech" are not expressing their anger at selected groups and categories in general, but at what they consider to be the "less desirable" people in Sweden, due to the mass immigration policy. There is also a class perspective built in. Had the outraged citizens refined their language and expressed their outrage in a more linguistically elegant way, they would not have been prosecuted. Imagine a Nazi and a university professor of political science saying exactly the same thing under the same circumstances about refugee policy, for example. I'm pretty sure only the Nazi would be convicted of incitement to hatred. In other words, it matters who says something.

Above all, the judgments are warnings to citizens: *Even if you don't like the immigration policy being pursued, beware of making your opinion public.* In everyday English: *Shut up!* Thus, the judgments narrow freedom of expression. That makes them political.

The politicians started with talking about hate speech against people of the same skin colour — which are also covered by the offence of incitement to racial hatred. They ended up in what is usually called an ideology of victimisation or victimhood. The law claims, for example, that black people are violated by the term "negro." However, there is nothing inherently offensive about the term, which simply means a person with black skin. What makes the term disgraceful is that we have decided that it refers to particularly well-known historical discrimination against black people. Furthermore, which is important not to forget, desecration is about experience. If the person using the term does not intend to defame the other and the person being called a negro does not feel defamed, then no defamation has taken place either. The consequence: there is no crime!

The incitement itself (the threat, the desecration) must always be reduced to the act itself (the deed) to convict someone. When you don't know who has committed a crime, no one can be convicted. For example, it is not possible to convict the Italian Mafia collectively for all the crimes it has committed. It should also be the case that when we do not find anyone who is affected, then no crime has been committed.

The hate-speech-legislation grants certain rights to groups and categories. I cannot understand this other than as an error in thinking. Rights and protections should be linked to individuals, not to ethnic, religious or sexual groups, any more than to pigment content. In a legal sense, the collective does not exist. It is individuals who are convicted of crimes and what they have done results in victims of crime, real flesh and blood people too. Exceptions are all those crimes that are directed against the politically agreed rules of a democratic society, such as traffic offences.

It is legally directly offensive that the constitutional freedom of expression is put at risk. The hate-speech-legislation is clearly political, both in its design and in practice.

## Legally, Muslims Are an Ethnic Group

There are approximately three billion Muslims in the world, who share a strong unifying religious bond across national borders. The number of Swedes is ten million. This makes Muslims undoubtedly Sweden's largest minority. Worldwide, there are 300 Muslims for every Swede.

Three days before Christmas Eve 2020, the Supreme Court ruled that a then 28-year-old man, who in January 2018 in the Facebook group *Politikfakta* wrote "Disgusting Muslim bastard," was guilty of incitement to hatred against a group of people. The comment was linked to an article about a man of foreign descent who allegedly committed an honour-related rape. The post itself was shared around 390 times and received around 1,300 reactions and 160 comments.

The wording should of course be read for what it is: an outraged comment on a shameful crime. One can strive for "good morals and good language" without dragging people to court for something they write online in a fit of passion. So said the man, who explained that he wrote the comment in anger at the perpetrator and that it was directed only at that person. The justices did not make it that easy. This is what the Supreme Court wrote, upholding the Court of Appeal's conviction:

> The 28-year-old's way of expressing himself in the comment, combined with the fact that it was made in immediate connection with the article, can according to the Supreme Court "not be understood in any other way than that (the 28-year-old) meant that the man's crime was directly linked to his supposed religious beliefs as a Muslim." Thus, the comment conveyed a "derogatory message that Muslims in general are prone to commit a certain type of serious crime. In addition, the Court held, the comment otherwise "undoubtedly expressed disdain for the group of Muslims within the meaning of the provision on incitement to hatred. [...] In light of this, the Supreme Court concludes that the comment cannot be understood as directed solely at the man in the article, "but also constituted a communication within the meaning of the criminal provision on incitement to hatred against a group of people." It was an "offensive value judgment which clearly exceeded the limits of objective criticism and debate.[12]

One of the three justices reported a dissenting opinion. He dismissed the indictment because he recognised its implications for freedom of expression:

> The assessment of the detailed meaning must be based on the fact that the criminal statute constitutes a restriction on the constitutionally protected freedom of expression. According to the Government's form, this freedom may not be restricted more than is necessary to achieve the ultimate objective that is to justify the restriction.

---

12   https://www.domstol.se/hogsta-domstolen/avgoranden/2020/87891/.

Unfortunately, that's how moral laws work. Legally, it was certainly correct that the man was convicted, but the political consequences are frightening. As one comment on *Flashback* puts it:

> Practically speaking there is not a single Muslim stupid enough to think that he means all Muslims, but unfortunately politicians and the judiciary have decided that the religion of Islam should be protected at all costs, and uses the hate speech legislation to do so. It does nothing but make Muslims look like snowflakes, and contributes more to racism than anything the man in question could have said.[13]

## Rewarded for Ratting

The Internet Hate Investigator (Sw. *Näthatsgranskaren*) is a self-appointed informant group run by Tomas Åberg, formed in early 2017. Together with a friend who is a computer system developer, he created his own search program that finds words and phrases that may be suspected of constituting incitement to hatred, sedition and unlawful threats. They started by testing the application on Facebook. More people joined the work and today the team, according to their own information, consists of about 15 people, including police officers, system developers, lecturers, lawyers and social scientists. They also already take the person's location, email address, etc. and submit complete information to the police.

A person who has been in Tomas Åberg's vicinity for many years is convinced that his purpose is twofold: to gain attention and to earn easy money through grants and subsidies.

In total, the Net Hate Reviewer has received 2.1 million SEK in government funding from the Swedish Agency for Youth and Civil Society (MUCF). Most of the money granted has been used for Tomas Åberg's own salary. When the project started, Tomas Åberg

13   https://www.flashback.org/p74036534.

was employed as a research assistant at Linköping University and received his salary from there.[14]

It is remarkable that an authority should support a private investigator doing police work in this way. This criticism that also affects the police, who have often, without further examination, taken Tomas Åberg's investigations and passed them on to prosecutors.

Already in the first year, Tomas Åberg and his colleagues made 750 reports. 14% of the cases went on to prosecution and 77 prosecutions ended in a conviction. In 2019, the number of convictions increased to over 300.[15] Many of those caught in Åberg's search program and reported for hate speech are old ladies who have written outrageous posts on Facebook about immigration to Sweden.

In 2018, the tabloid *Aftonbladet* nominated Tomas Åberg as one of eight *Swedish heroes* for his work against "right-wing extremist online hate," because he "demonstrated courage, civil courage and humanity." In other words, he would be rewarded for the same kind of persecution that was carried out in Nazi Germany, the Soviet Union and East Germany.

Together with other local politicians in the south of Sweden a social democratic feminist wrote that it is now time to classify pornography as hate speech against women:

> … women are still murdered in Sweden every year because they are women. Therefore, we from Skåne, as well as the women's and girls' organisation Unizon, want the penalties for crimes with sexist and mi-sogynistic motives to be tightened and classified as hate crimes. This will make it clear that such crimes are part of a structural problem and not individual incidents or figures in the statistics. We also believe that the killing of women by men should be classified as femicide when the motive is precisely misogyny. This makes it clear in the statistics that the motive behind

---

14  https://www.ingridochmaria.se/2020/10/08/nathatsgranskaren-anvander-rattsvasendet-som-ett-pyramidspel/.

15  https://uvell.se/2018/03/06/nathatsgranskaren-och-valet/.

the crimes is precisely misogyny. We also believe that pornography should be classified as incitement to hatred against women.[16]

I toy with the idea that pornography also falls under the hate speech legislation. What possibilities that would open up for Tomas Åberg, who boasts of 300 convictions! How many can there be if he also gets the opportunity to hang porn producers by his scalp belt? I can't find any figures on the industry's turnover in Sweden, but globally it is said to be close to a thousand billion SEK, however you measure it.

Claiming to be a non-profit activity, the online investigator is in fact a business idea that exploits the justice system, since a police report must be investigated and if it is passed on to the prosecutor, the latter is obliged to prosecute, if the criteria are met. The judiciary has no real means of sorting out the charges to be brought. The investigator's reporting activities therefore complicate and delay the judicial system's ability to deal with more serious and socially threatening crime.

## The Truth Is Illegal

In 2010, Dutch party leader Geert Wilders was brought before a court on charges of racism and hate crimes. He wanted to ban the Koran, claiming, among other things, that Islam is a totalitarian ideology. Witnesses were called to back up his claims. The prosecutor said it was irrelevant whether Wilders's witnesses could prove that Wilders's observations were correct. Regardless, his observations were illegal. In other words, the prosecutor claimed that the truth may be unlawful. Obviously, he got his point across, because Geert Wilders was convicted.

On 7 October, Nyköping District Court convicted a Sweden Democrat politician of incitement to hatred. In a statement to the regional council, he had claimed that South Sudanese had a low IQ

---

16   https://www.sydsvenskan.se/2019-08-13/klassa-pornografi-som-hets-mot-folkgrupp-mot-kvinnor.

and that they would therefore have difficulty finding work in Sweden. In the trial, he argued that the criticism was not directed against the Southern Sudanese but against Swedish politicians.

There is a strong parallel here with the judgment against Geert Wilders, in that the district court never examined whether the allegation was true or not. Bertil Malmberg was sentenced to a suspended sentence and to pay a fine of 24,000 SEK. The district court considered it derogatory to claim that South Sudanese are less worthy than others.

Despite being convicted, the politician stood by his claim, for the simple reason that, supported by the available research, he was convinced that it was true. However, the group leader of the region's Sweden Democrats was not on his side and said that the language was unacceptable.

In June 2021, the politician was asked to resign from his political post and in early November of the same year he was expelled. He commented "It's sad. After all the years that I have put into the party and then being mistreated in this way, I don't think it's fair."[17]

It is frightening that in none of the cases mentioned above is the court even interested in trying to find out what is true. This is outside the court's remit, even though the claim that Islam is a totalitarian ideology is entirely correct, as is the claim that South Sudanese have a significantly lower intelligence than Swedes — with the addition that it is not possible in the individual case to judge a person's intelligence, based on race or ethnicity.

Intelligence tests and the concept of IQ are scientifically the best designed and most robust measurement tools in psychology. If you don't accept IQ research, then you might as well skip psychology altogether.

IQ tests are based on a normal value of 100, with those below that average having lower intelligence and those above having higher. That

17   https://www.svt.se/nyheter/lokalt/sormland/bertil-malmberg-sd-kommer-att-sitta-kvar.

some people possess higher intelligence is not controversial knowledge; moreover, we find it quite easy to admire such individuals (e.g. Einstein, what a genius!). To acknowledge Silicon Valley, with its IQ average of over 130 for those involved in developing computers and software, is not controversial, at least not in terms of intelligence. And Mensa, which is an association for people with high intelligence, has a collection of rather odd members, but is in no way politically compromised. We can also mention that Ashkenazi Jews, together with the inhabitants of Hong Kong and Singapore, rank highest in the world without questioning the measurements.

On the other hand, those who fall below the limit are problematic. Then the criticism of intelligence tests comes like a letter on the post. It runs along two lines. One is that the tests are designed to favour Westerners. The question then is why it is Asians and not Westerners who come out on top. The other criticises heredity and points to poverty and hunger as the explanation for the low intelligence of some countries. Neither of these claims holds up very well, scientifically speaking.

In their research report *IQ and Global Inequality* (2002) English psychologist Richard Lynn and Finnish political scientist Tatu Vanhanen show that that intelligence, as measured by IQ tests, has a high explanatory power in terms of national wealth and social well-being. They base this argument on the finding that the average IQ of nations has a strong correlation with factors such as higher education (0.75), life expectancy (0.77) and democratisation (0.57). Four years later they published another report *IQ and the Wealth of Nations,* in which they respond to the criticisms levelled at the earlier book. To show that IQ measures are highly reliable, they compare the results for two different measurement methods and 71 countries.

The correlation between different approaches to measuring national IQ is as high as 0.95. As a further argument for reliability, they state that reported national IQs are correlated with various measures of mathematics and science achievement. They correlate from 0.79 to 0.89.

In an interview in a Finnish magazine in 2004, Tatu Vanhanen claimed that while the average intelligence of Finns is 97, in Africa it is between 60 and 70. He also said that the main explanation for Africa's poverty was precisely low intelligence. This almost started a public campaign in Finland against him, but he survived because he had not added any values. In his studies of democracy, which was the focus of his research, Vanhanen concluded that it did not seem possible to build a democracy in a country with an average IQ below 90. Danish researcher Helmuth Nyborg also argued this, which led to him being stripped of his emeritus title. Empirically, the claim is true, but it is by no means impossible for a country with a very low measured IQ to build a democracy. One concept used in IQ psychology is *smart fraction*, which applies to the part of the tested collective that is above 108 and thus, in another psychological concept, has *cognitive capital*. Of course, if this is the category in power in a country, a society with an average score below 90 can have a functioning democracy.

However, they are less likely to be able to build a welfare state, as this requires well-educated citizens who can compete with their services and products in a global market. In Sweden, the number of university graduates is as high as 44% of the working-age population.

If countries where the population has an average IQ below ninety are unable to build attractive democratic societies, is it a good idea to import people from such countries to Sweden? Even if it may be morally offensive, it is politically reasonable to reject economic migrants who will almost certainly have to be supported for the rest of their lives with Swedish taxpayers' money. In addition, they are clearly over-represented in crime. It is part of our political responsibility to make controversial, though necessary, decisions.

More important than drawing out these arguments, however, is for politicians and other decision-makers to understand how human

intelligence varies. Ultimately, this is about taking responsibility
for both democracy and the welfare society. This does not apply to
those who are truly refugees, but it does apply to those who come to
Sweden from other parts of the world and other cultures in search of
a better life. We should not completely refrain from choosing those to
whom we want to give this top prize in the migration raffle.

# The Contempt for Swedes

## A Form of Integration

POLITICIANS LIKE to talk about the importance of *integrating* immigrants. Usually, they do not define their terms. They take it for granted that to 'integrate' foreigners means successfully adapting them to Swedish society, i.e. providing for themselves and their families, not being criminals and affirming Swedish values. For me, integration basically means no more than a form of adaptation. Immigrants have learned a Swedish life of some kind, but all the while as they continue to affirm their ethnic identity. That they are integrated means that they are not yet *assimilated*. Then, in what way they are integrated is not a moral but an empirical question.

The hatred and contempt for what Sweden is creates a community, as a kind of counter-image to the values that all good and right-thinking Swedes affirm. Even if it is not desired, it is a form of integration. The racism against Swedes that has formed over a long period of time is far more violent, more widespread and more politically and culturally sanctioned than the racism of Swedes against immigrants.

The headline also refers to the contempt of politicians and opinion-makers for their own people. Since this contempt, too, is directed against ethnic Swedes, it is reasonable to include it under the same heading: the contempt for Swedes.

In an email exchange, a Swedish philosopher writes to me that it is difficult for Swedish citizens to understand that the state is no longer on their side. He is not referring to pension commitments, unemployment benefits and the like, but to fundamental qualities such as border protection and legal certainty. These are commitments that the state will not naturally see as its task in the future. To put it bluntly: in the new world order, the state is obviously not in solidarity with the people. Below is a sample of what citizens can expect.

## Gotlandgate

For a long time, the island of Gotland was the least multicultural county in Sweden, something that local politicians managed to change. In 2012, the County Governor outlined her strategy to attract more immigrants to settle on Gotland and make the island *multicultural*, which for her was a positively charged concept. She argued that Gotland needed more immigrants to cope with jobs and welfare. She offered a "2Gotland package" that included special rights and benefits, including priority access to housing and job vacancies. As there is a shortage of both jobs and housing on the island, this was not something that delighted the Gotlanders. Her proposals were heavily criticised, with opponents arguing that there was no reason to allow politicians to turn Gotland into another Malmö, Södertälje or Bergsjön — areas that even the politicians who created them did not want to live in. They warned of asylum chaos.

According to the County Administrative Board's report, 660 asylum seekers were living on the island in July 2016. Most were placed in one of a total of seven facilities. Gotland's politicians had committed to receiving an additional 192 asylum seekers during the year. Approximately 200 unaccompanied "children" were living in institutions designed for children with social problems. At one point, the Gotland boat had transported as many as 200 asylum seekers to the island. They are said to have been scavenging in the restaurant and stealing like ravens from the shop. The staff, unable to stop it all, were told to keep quiet about the incident. Although the media were reluctant to report such incidents, word was spreading.

In Visby, Gotland's only city, accommodation for asylum seekers was opened in the Östercentrum quarter. In December 2015, a shop there was stormed by some 20 people from the asylum centre. They stole almost everything they could get their hands on. There were also reports that drug trafficking has become a major problem for the shops in Östercentrum. This led the shop owners to apply to become a so-called Paragraph 3 area, which meant more security guards with greater authority than ordinary guards. Such areas already existed in several other parts of the country, but for Gotland it was not considered necessary in the past.

There were also other reports that not all asylum seekers are God's best children. A 26-year-old woman from Gotland who organised a vigilante group of ordinary Gotlanders — In 2016 it had 800 members — said that the young men in the asylum accommodation would stand in the middle of the road and spit on the ground in front of you. If true, it was not the kind of behaviour that increased the newcomers' popularity with the locals.

At one point, two of the asylum-seeking men were beaten up. They told the police that the perpetrators were Swedes, but they managed to leave the scene before they were arrested. The police immediately went out with the description that the attackers were "very Swedish" and that they were "cowards," although they did not appear to be any more than the men who had been beaten. Had the situation been the other way round, that two asylum seekers had assaulted a couple of Swedes, one can be sure that the police would not have written that the attackers were "very foreign." Nor would they have been called cowards.

Until mid-October 2016, a total of 28 rapes had been reported on Gotland during the year. This was the reason for the creation of the vigilante group. They had taken on a single issue: safety for Gotland's women.

Social media called it a rape epidemic. Without being certain, all the perpetrators appeared to be immigrants. One of these rapes made the cup run over for the Gotlanders. It was a 33-year-old wheelchair-bound woman who was going home and shared a taxi with a man unknown to her. She went with him to the villa where he lived because she needed to borrow the toilet. There, she was raped by five or possibly six men, all of whom were asylum seekers. As the villa was a shelter, it is likely that several of them were legally classified as minor. The woman had no means of escape. Her lawyer said she was shocked, paralysed and feared for her life. That is why she did not even dare to try to resist. Finally, she had given in to the situation. She shut down. She went through this, only to, as she experienced it, come out alive.

After several hours, she was helped of the house and was able to call the police. According to the lawyer, she had to seek treatment for both physical and psychological injuries.

The police opened a preliminary investigation. The policeman who led the investigation was from Lebanon, where he was born in a refugee camp for Palestinian refugees, which almost certainly meant that he was a Muslim, as was probably the case for the men suspected of rape. Given how agitated and suspicious the Gotlanders were, this was not the ideal choice of investigator.

Now something unexpected happened, namely that the prosecutor released the men suspected of rape. He said that the act itself was not based on violence or threats, but on taking advantage of the special situation of the target. The woman's story was not so robust that it could easily be used as a basis for an arrest. It differed too much from the suspects' story. Although there were reasons to question their stories on some points as well.

The fact that the woman did not put up sufficient resistance should reasonably be of no significance, since she was in a wheelchair and could not get out of it on her own. The Criminal Code states that a person who commits rape is a person who carries out sexual intercourse or a sexual act with a person "by taking improper advantage of the fact that the person is in a particularly vulnerable situation due to unconsciousness, sleep, serious fear, intoxication or other drug influence, illness, bodily injury or mental disorder or otherwise in view of the circumstances."

If one is wheelchair bound, is in a toilet and is attacked by five/ six people, how can that be interpreted in any other way than that the woman is in a "particularly vulnerable situation"? How she then acts herself should be irrelevant. There is no requirement that she should scream or resist.

When the men were released, there were outraged comments on Facebook. A hundred angry Gotlanders gathered at the villa where the suspects were staying. It was just a block away from the police station. Not much else happened. Some of them proceeded to the home of the prosecutor, where they don't seem to have done anything special, other than gather outside.

A carpenter, member of the Nordic Resistance movement, filmed the men who were probably the perpetrators and posted the film online. As a result, the following morning he was searched by the police and arrested. Earlier in the week he had been harassed by police who stopped his work van to force him to take a drug test. The police refused to say what he was suspected of. For what reason was he arrested? It's quite possible that an ambitious prosecutor could get his recording of the suspected rapists and spin it as an "unlawful threat" or some kind of violation, although that seems far-fetched.

About ten activists of the Nordic resistance movement went to the island and organised a demonstration. For the media, the presence of this extreme group on Gotland was welcome. If the protests escalated, they could spin it to mean that the uprising was directed and organised by Nazis. But most of all, they wanted to keep as low a profile as possible. In the local newspaper *Hela Gotland*, you could read: "Around 14:30 reports came in that there had been a minor clash between the protesters and passers-by which meant that the police had to intervene." What happened was that an immigrant gang challenged the activists of the Nordic Resistance Movement and wanted them to go to another place and settle.

The activists replied that they were not hooligans and that if the immigrants wanted to fight, they could attack them on the spot.

The Gotland police requested reinforcements from the mainland, as they felt they were unable to handle the situation. The situation was classified as a "special event." A special event usually involves riots, terrorism or bomb threats. What did the police fear the Gotlanders would do? An extra police force was sent to Gotland, not to protect Gotland women from being raped, but to protect the prosecutors and the judiciary. These police officers were trained for violent situations, such as demonstrations and riots. On the internet, it was said that when people get upset and start protesting, the police have the resources to quell the "riot." About the task force it is written sarcastically on the net: "Have they solved the crime of rape, then? Or was it more important to harass ten Nazis in the pouring rain?"

The chairman of the Social Democratic Party of the Regional Council said, "There are dark forces at work and that worries me. We have to talk based on facts and not on rumours. Now we have to show civil courage and stand up to the values and attitudes that are coming."

The County Governor said: "It is deeply unfortunate what is happening. We have to ensure that the rule of law functions properly. We cannot take the law into our own hands. We need wise citizens now."

A feminist member of the island council said: "What has happened is terrible and I want to give all my support to the victim. The reality is that this type of crime is not increasing, and that it is men of different ethnicities who are responsible for the violence. The problem is a destructive male norm, not a particular ethnicity or culture."

An outraged backlash took off online. A business owner in western Sweden contacted at journalist at the online TV channel *SwebbTV* and said he would like to ease the pain of the raped woman. Maybe she wanted to travel somewhere, spend time elsewhere? He wanted to donate 25,000 SEK. This led a journalist at *SwebbTV* to start a fundraising campaign using alternative media and in almost no time at all he raised 115,000 SEK from over five hundred donors, in addition to the promised 25,000 SEK from the businessman. This could, of course, be a topic for the media to report on, but that's not how it works — not in Sweden.

At first, the media reported in the form of short notices, but when the resistance grew into a local revolt on Gotland, it was not possible to continue to keep the Swedish people in the dark. Apart from the alternative media, nowhere in the media coverage did it appear that this was an occasion when there was reason for newsrooms and journalists to, if not exactly side with the citizens, then to be careful about neutral reporting. No journalists explained that the police were doing the same thing as in totalitarian countries, they were turning against the population. Sweden's journalists, seemingly without reflection and as a matter of course, sided with the powers that be. An editorial in the local paper *Gotlands Folkblad* warned that the boot-stomping of the Browns would soon be heard on "our Gotland streets."

On Friday, 14 October, the media could no longer keep quiet. In *Svenska Dagbladet*, law professor Mårten Schultz wrote under the headline "Scary threats to prosecutors." He touched briefly on the rape that sparked the Gotlanders' revolt. He wrote: "The background to the events is that a disabled woman reported that she had been raped by several men." He then linked this, the fact that Gotlanders had gathered outside the prosecutor's residence, to threats against prosecutors by professional criminals. He goes on to compare this to the attacks on police, ambulance and fire men in the so-called vulnerable suburbs, or ethnic areas. This was not only ignorant but also deeply indecent.

*Dagens Nyheter* went one step further in its editorial of the same day. Under the headline "Dissolve the lynch mob" they call the Gotlanders a mob and the protests a hate storm. Then they wrote, and please note, this does not refer to the rape of the wheelchair-bound woman but to the popular protests: "The events on Gotland are disgusting and unacceptable but unfortunately not surprising. It is not the first time we have seen this type of lynch mob in suspected sex crimes."

About ordinary people having had enough they say: "It is a disgusting, extremely ominous development. Who are these ordinary people? Why are they acting in the name of other Swedes?"

The unnamed editorial writer concludes by warning that "this kind of incitement can end in people dying." A clearer sign that the authorities are the enemy of the people is hard to come by.

The Sweden Democrats also sided with the government on this issue. Their group leader in the Gotland council, distanced himself from the Citizens' Guard. Note that it was ordinary Gotlanders who patrolled the streets of Visby at night because they felt that the police were not doing their job.

On Sunday 16 October 2016, Feminist Initiative and the Left Party organised a demonstration. On Facebook, they called the over-representation of immigrants as sex offenders a "mystified threat from outside" that is a "simplified description of reality." For them, rape was a man's problem, which must surely be seen as an even more far-fetched simplification. Participants were lured to the manifestation with the following text: "Today we all show racists and sexists that we are many, strong and that we stand up for the equal value of all. There will be torches and music. Speeches will be given by […] and the text above will be read in Romanian, Somali, Dari, Persian, Arabic and Kurdish. Anyone who shares values with the spirit of the demonstration is welcome! "

It's very hard to understand how they had the nerve to claim they were representing women. After all, they did not represent any women's interests, but instead sided with the perpetrators. They were the ones to be pitied.

Around 300 people attended, many of them travelling from the mainland. The media coverage never questioned the good and right of this demonstration. A priest was interviewed on the radio. He was outraged by the sexual behaviour of men, especially Swedish men. He had been threatened on the Internet. Now good and right-thinking Swedes must stand up to the dark forces.

"Gotlandgate" is far from the only example of how a racist attack on a Swedish woman leads to so-called anti-racist demonstrations. In the northern Swedish town of Bollnäs, an eighteen-year-old girl was gang-raped by an Afro-Arab immigrant gang. They beat her severely while raping her. The rape was so brutal that she was unconscious for parts of the event. This led to anti-racist demonstrations against the Sweden Democrats and the racism of Swedes against immigrants.[1]

Another example of disgusting reactions was when a toddler's father was, completely unprovoked, beaten to death on his way home from a Christmas party. Dalarna Against Racism and other so-called anti-racists showed up and demonstrated against the Sweden Democrats and "racism" under slogans such as "No racists on our streets" and "*Jalla jalla* — Sweden for all!."[2]

As stated in an elaborate essay from 2016, posted anonymously online and entitled "Swedish whores":

> If there is one conclusion to be drawn, superior to all others, it is that Swedish anti-racism is intellectually dishonest, genuinely hateful and neurotic, and that in its quest to make things better for one group it makes things worse not only for that group, but also for everyone else — except, of course, the minority of immigrants who are given free pass after free pass, no matter what crimes they commit and why they commit them. Swedish so-called anti-racism is based on delusions, false facts, biased reports and a huge deficit of seriously conducted scientific research; it is based on wishful thinking, a desire to portray the world as it might have been rather than as it is; it is based on inbred backslapping and threats of adult bullying.[3]

---

1   http://www.helahalsingland.se/halsingland/bollnas/ordnar-manifestation-mot-rasism,    http://www.friatider.se/svensk-flicka-gruppvaldtagen-av-invandrare-da-anordnas-manifestation-mot-rasism.

2   https://www.nordfront.se/fa-kom-till-antirasistiskt-mote-i-ludvika.smr, https://www.flashback.org/t1743761.

3   https://svennehora.wordpress.com/.

## The Humiliation Robberies

Robberies involving violence and humiliation have become almost commonplace in some parts of the country. Many robbers have been so young that they have been sentenced to community service, which has in effect enabled them to commit new crimes after having already been convicted — often repeatedly.

In December 2021, the Crime Prevention Council published a report showing a doubling of youth robberies between 2015 and 2019. In total, 3,274 people were suspected of one or more robberies, and 7,909 young people have reported being the victim of a robbery. Expensive jackets, more expensive mobile phones, and wireless headphones are popular items for young "Swedish" thieves. Victims do not live in the same socially deprived areas as the perpetrators. They live in more affluent areas, but the robberies are not committed there or in the perpetrators' home areas. It happens in more neutral places, such as near schools, shopping centres, or other meeting places.[4] Police statistics also show that cases of children being robbed have doubled in three years.

- 66% of the suspected robbers are of foreign origin.

- 12% of robbers with Swedish background have a parent born abroad.

- Among the victims, 77% have Swedish background.

- When boys and girls rob together, it is mainly boys who are the victims.

- When girls are also involved, it is more common for the robberies to be filmed.

- Where only girls have been suspects, the victims are of the same sex in 92% of cases.

---

4    https://bra.se/publikationer/arkiv/publikationer/2021-12-15-ungdomsran.html.

- The number of girl robbers increases and are more brutal with excessive violence, demonstrations of power and humiliation.

The motives for youth robbery are usually the need for money, status within the group, excitement, or an underlying conflict between the suspect and the victim. Almost half of all youth robberies are committed by a person who has been suspected of youth robbery at least once before. The proportion of girls suspected of juvenile robbery has increased from 4–8% between 2015 and 2019. The increase is particularly marked in the Stockholm police region. The tabloid *Expressen* gives some examples:

> A robbery gang drove around with a boy in southern Stockholm and forced him to withdraw money from an ATM. They also urinated in his mouth and filmed the assault.
>
> In several other cases, the robbers also forced their victims to kiss their feet and the videos were shared on social media.
>
> Another gang forced its victim to "crawl like a pig" while filming.[5]

Those who have been robbed and humiliated feel bad afterwards; several of the parents of victims interviewed also report fear and anxiety, both for themselves and their children. The children want to be home early in the evening; they are afraid of bumping into one of the perpetrators and they even want to move out. Several of the parents indicated that they would have needed more support in their parental role.

One of these humiliating robberies stand out, particularly for its cruelty. On the night of 22–23 August 2020, two Swedish boys, aged 15 and 16, were on their way home from a party. But 18-year-old Mohamed-Amin El Hani and 21-year-old Ali Jahani Asl stopped them and wanted to sell drugs. When the boys refused, they were taken at knifepoint to Solna cemetery. They were forced to act

---

5    https://www.expressen.se/kronikorer/fredrik-sjoshult/flickornas-fornedring-sran-brutalt-vald-som-filmas-/.

friendly and hold their tormentors so as not to arouse the suspicions of any witnesses that something was wrong.

The robbers took away the boys' valuables and demanded the ATM-code to their Visa cards, to get more out of the robbery. But it didn't stop there: the Swedish boys were forced by the perpetrators into open graves. There they had to take off their clothes, and the perpetrators put socks in their mouths so they could not scream. They were stabbed and beaten with both shovels and sticks. They were threatened to have their penises and ears cut off, their noses would be smashed, etc. They were burned with lighters and one of them was raped and urinated on. At one point during the night, they were forced into separate pits to be buried alive. They froze to the point of shaking, where they were forced to lie naked against the earth. The cold almost surpassed the pain of the many blows and kicks they received. One of the boys said afterwards that he had given up hope and thought he was going to die. After receiving death threats and beatings throughout the night, the boys finally managed to escape in the morning, when the perpetrators turned their backs on them.

Mohamed-Amin El Hani and Ali Jahani Asl were arrested the same day near the cemetery. One of them had several of the victim's belongings on him. Both robbers were known, as they had previously committed robberies before in Solna. One of them was serving a sentence for arson at the time of the rape robbery but went free.

The District Court sentenced the 18-year-old to five years in prison. The 21-year-old was sentenced to nine years. They were also jointly ordered to pay damages to the teenagers, more than 250,000 SEK to one boy and almost 145,000 SEK to the other.

The boys who were robbed described during the trial how the hours in the cemetery changed them. One of them felt remorse for having persuaded the other to walk home in the summer night and how he had become afraid of being outside. He had trouble eating and sleeping. The other boy told the court that his schoolwork was going badly and that at night he woke up in a cold sweat from nightmares.

## The Hatred of Swedes

The question is whether the persecution and abuse of Swedes by immigrants is a more vicious social problem than the racism committed by ethnic Swedes. However, both lawyers and politicians have turned a deaf ear to this. A foreigner or an immigrant can say or write almost anything to or about ethnic Swedes, without being prosecuted. As one *Flashback* writer notes, "Go on any Arab forum and it's not that people are talking about disgusting insults, but much worse about us Swedes. But no one cares, because no one checks there."

In 2003, a columnist in a free Stockholm newspaper claimed that "Swedes are the most boring, stupid, mean and silly people I have ever met." A private individual reported the newspaper for incitement to hatred against Swedes. The then Chancellor of Justice dropped the case on the following grounds:

> The aim of the criminal law on incitement to hatred was to ensure legal protection for minority groups of different compositions and believers of different faiths. The case of someone expressing criticism of Swedes was probably not intended to be covered by the criminal statute.[6]

Seven years later, the next Chancellor of Justice said much the same thing, after a newspaper had been reported to the police for the claim that "the Swede is the greatest handicap of our time." Again, the Chancellor of Justice refrained from opening an investigation. The reason given was that criticism of Swedes "was not intended to be covered by the criminal statute." She cited the earlier Chancellor of Justice's decision as justification. In 2013, journalist wrote in in the magazine *ICA-kuriren*:

---

6    https://www.jk.se/beslut-och-yttranden/2003/11/3217-03-30/.

> The purest are of course the peoples who have isolated themselves for
> generations and only marry each other. They sit there severely inbred with
> drooping chins, severe genetic diseases and an IQ of 70.[7]

The piece was meant to be an attack on Sweden Democrats, but it was
unclear whether the statement was aimed at Swedes or some other
ethnic group. In at least three decisions, the Chancellor of Justice has
thus ruled that Swedes should not be protected by the law on incitement against ethnic groups.

The Parliament Justice Committee has taken a different line and
interpreted incitement to hatred as applying equally to ethnic Swedes
as to other ethnic groups. This has been argued on several occasions,
whenever the Sweden Democrats have proposed a review of the law.
However, no one has ever been convicted of incitement against ethnic
groups, that is, when it has been incitement against Swedes. In March
2014, a 24-year-old from Stockholm, who described himself as a Jew
and a socialist, wrote on his blog:

> Swedes are the worst of the goyim. Swedes are a people who have
> never been able to behave in a civilized manner, but have barbarism pro-
> grammed into their genes. This leads to the fact that almost every Swede
> is a potential sexual offender, and to the fact that Swedes have no respect
> for Jews and others. Swedes behave like animals. I would go so far as to
> say that Swedes — both ethnic and cultural Swedes — compared to other
> peoples, are vermin, disgusting vermin. It would be only right if all Swedes
> were exterminated — disappeared from the face of the earth.

It is a perfect example of incitement against a group of people, even
if one starts from the first narrow wording from 1948. The man who
wrote the text also promised that anyone who could prove that he
had committed a crime would receive 25,000 SEK. A non-profit association, Spiritvs Neronis, sued him, but the District Court turned the
case into a civil suit, which the man won. The court declared that the
limit for incitement to hatred should be set higher for Swedes than

---

7    http://www.icakuriren.se/Diskutera-F...riktig-svensk/.

for other ethnic groups: "The need to restrict freedom of expression in relation to statements directed at majority groups would not, in the opinion of the district court, be as great as in relation to minority groups." And further: "However, the nature of the statement seems to be such that it can best be dealt with in a free and open debate." The dissident paper *Nya Tider* writes:

> Since the ruling, many commentators have pointed out that the Norrköping District Court's ruling maintains the double standard whereby the Swedish majority population is considered less worthy of protection than other ethnic groups. If it is not enough to write that a certain ethnic group is a disgusting vermin and deserves to be exterminated — how can anyone be convicted of incitement against this ethnic group at all?[8]

In 2019, a Sweden Democrat politician wrote an interpellation entitled "Hate crimes against Swedes." Now it was not just about hate expressed online and in the mainstream media, but about outright abuse. He addressed the Social Democrat and Minister of Justice, Morgan Johansson:

> When the victim was unable to withdraw money on his card, the young robbers became disgruntled and punished him by showering him with kicks. A film of the incident began circulating in mid-December, and the 16-year-olds have now been sentenced. The beating ends with them saying "disgusting fucking Swede" and forcing him to open his mouth so they can urinate in it. This is just one of countless files circulating online where youth gangs abuse other youths in what can only be described as hate crimes.

> The problem has now grown so large that it affects a whole generation of Swedish teenagers, young men and women who constantly have to consider the fact that they can be beaten and robbed because they are Swedish by origin.

> Every year, a number of reports are made in which the victims are suspected of being selected because they are Swedish. Hate crime is not

8    https://www.nyatider.nu/skyddas-svenskar-av-hmf-lagen/.

a separate category of crime, but a penalty that is increased because the perpetrator wanted to offend the victim based on who the victim is. It is about the person's religion, skin colour, sexual orientation, origin or ethnicity. If the prosecutor manages to prove that someone is abusing someone else because they are dark-skinned, the punishment is harsher. But this should also apply if it is proven that the victim was victimised because he or she is Swedish. But so far there are no convictions when victims are selected because they are Swedish, and even the prosecutors do not know how to prosecute cases. […]

In other words, a distinction is made here on the origin. Hate crimes against a person of Swedish origin are not considered as serious because the person of Swedish origin belongs to a majority overall in the country.[9]

As expected, Minister of Justice Morgan Johansson replied by referring to the Justice Committee and that nothing in the legislation says that Swedes are not also protected by the law. "So, I don't see that the current provisions would discriminate against Swedes." However, he deftly avoided the statement that there are no convictions for hate crimes against Swedes. He also counter-attacked, claiming that this was all about the Sweden Democrats' hostility to immigrants and desire to split Sweden's different ethnic groups.

That's cleverly worded. And disgusting, too. What kind of lawyers and politicians do we have who do not want to protect their own population?

---

9    https://www.riksdagen.se/sv/dokument-lagar/dokument/interpellation/hat-brott-mot-svenskar_H710351.

# The Future

## Deprived Areas

I N 2004, the Liberal Party's then spokesperson on integration
made what was called a Map of Areas of Special Deprivation. The
criteria for being defined as a particularly deprived area were:

- fewer than 60% of working-age residents were in employment
  and

- the percentage of pupils having completed primary education was
  below 70%

- or the percentage of eligible voters who voted in the last municipal elections was below 70% (or both).

By 1990, Sweden had three such areas that met the criteria. Twelve
years later, no less than 136 neighbourhoods were classified as areas
of Special Deprivation. By 2006, the number had grown to 156 areas.[1]
The Liberal Party then abandoned the project.

On behalf of a think tank, a respected researcher updated the map
in 2012. Then there were 186 deprived areas in Sweden. 566,000 people lived in these areas. This was an increase of 16% compared to the
figure for 2006.[2]

---

1   https://www.dn.se/debatt/allt-fler-far-det-allt-samre-i-utsatta-bostadsom-
    raden/.

2   https://www.dnv.se/nyheter/ny-rapport-utanforskapets-karta-en-uppfoljning-
    av-folkpartiets-rapportserie/.

## Riots

On May 9th, 2013, a 69-year-old man was shot dead by police in a suburb west of Stockholm. The incident was assessed as self-defence. It was the spark that ignited a riot in which at least 100 vehicles were set on fire. The centre was also vandalised, and a garage was set on fire, forcing the evacuation of nearby residents. Police were met with stone-throwing, and three police officers were injured. The police estimated that 50–60 youths were involved. However, no arrests were made that night.

The disturbances continued the following evening. Eleven cars and four containers were set on fire, and stones were thrown at police and emergency services. Seven police officers were injured. Police estimate that 50 to 100 people were involved, some as young as 12 or 13.

There were also riots in many other suburbs around Stockholm. Thirty cars were set on fire and the police station in Jakobsberg as well as the shopping centre there were vandalised. In Rågsved the police station was set on fire and in Hagsätra, one policeman was injured. In Skogås a restaurant was set on fire, and firemen were attacked with stones.

Young people also threw stones and bottles at Vällingby metro station. They smashed the windows of several metro trains and threatened the staff before leaving the station. At least two schools, a police station, and 15 cars were burnt down. During the riots, 32 police officers were injured.

In February 2017, a Monday evening, the police were about to arrest a wanted person at the metro station in the Stockholm suburb of Rinkeby. They were pelted with stones but managed to arrest the wanted man and get away. A couple of hours later, a riot started and about ten cars were set on fire. Shops were looted and a shopkeeper was beaten up. A newspaper photographer was assaulted and a person on his way home was both beaten and robbed. The fire brigade tried to enter the area but were also pelted with stones and had to retreat. The next day, the police managed to restore calm. One of the consequences was that two bus lines no longer stop at five stops, including Rinkeby centre.

Five hours before the riots, Donald Trump singled out Sweden as a horror story. As a result, the riots became international news. American journalist Tim Pool made his way to Sweden and Rinkeby, where he was followed by young, masked men who threatened him. He wrote on Twitter that he thought he could walk around areas without problems, but he was wrong. There is a video posted on YouTube with 145,000 views, in which he says: "I am sorry Sweden, but I find you creepy."[3]

In April 2022, the Danish politician and anti-Islam activist Rasmus Paludan, chairman of the small political party Strict Direction (Sw. *Stram Kurs*), sought permission for several demonstrations with Koran burning in Sweden. The aim was to demonstrate the Swedish government's failure to integrate immigrants, while at the same time testing the limits of free speech in Sweden.

Here it should be noted that the Koran which Rasmus Paludan burnt was his own copy, which is protected by the freedom of expression that is enshrined in the Swedish constitution. It is on the same level as if he burned a novel by Joyce Carol Oates. He may do so, however provoked Joyce Carol Oates would be. The same with the Bible and the Torah.

On 14 April 2022, Paludan burned a Koran in Råslätt, a suburb of Jönköping, without causing any disturbances. To disrupt, the priest Fredrik Hollertz rang the church bells. Later in the day, another Koran burning was planned in suburb to Linköping. The riot started before Paludan turned up, forcing him to cancel his demonstration. Some very upset Muslims broke up paving stones before the police arrived. The riot grew larger and more violent. Many were injured

---

3   https://www.youtube.com/watch?v=4Sbl7SkHZTs.

and police vehicles were set on fire. Children and mothers also then took part in the stone-throwing against the police.

In Rinkeby, violence broke out the day after and here also police officers had stones thrown at them. In Örebro, Paludan planned to burn a Koran the same day. This led to another violent riot and many people were injured. Around ten police cars were damaged, several of which were set on fire. In addition, a police car was hijacked and driven around by masked men.

On 16 April, two gatherings were planned. Violence broke out at both locations. Several cars were set on fire, and stones were thrown at police officers. In Malmö, a school was set on fire and a Molotov cocktail was thrown at a city bus. Passengers were forced to flee.

A total of no less than 183 police officers were reportedly injured during the riots, sixteen of them so seriously that they had to take sick leave. A female police officer was hit in the head with a stone. As she fell to the ground, the mob laughed and continued to throw stones at the prone woman. This kind of mindless, bloodthirsty barbarism had never been seen by the police before. There were many such testimonies.

The Christian Democrat party leader said the police should have fired live ammunition at the demonstrators. She argued that it was a topsy turvy world when over 100 police officers were injured. It should have been over a hundred rioters who were injured instead.

These riots attracted international attention. Rasmus Paludan's provocation had the effect he wanted it to have. Strong condemnations came from Muslim countries: Iran, Iraq, Indonesia, Pakistan, the United Arab Emirates and Saudi Arabia. Muslims demonstrated outside the Swedish embassy in Teheran, Iran. A diplomat from China demanded that the Swedish government respected the religions of minorities.

The debate came down to whether Paludan's activism was to be seen as expression of freedom or incitement to hatred. But it was also clear that the stone-throwers were not fighting with Paludan, who they didn't know, but with the police.

The recurring riots were not about Koran burning but about the fact that we have parallel societies in Sweden where Swedish law is not recognised. They show parallel structures of norms and lawlessness in our segregated suburbs, which can turn in an instant into ruthless violence against police officers, ambulance staff, and ordinary people. This happens at the same time as news updates tick in about new shootings and deaths in the ongoing gang wars.

It is not Paludan's fault that Sweden has citizens who hate Sweden, Swedes, and especially Swedish police. The consequence is that the perpetrators of violence experience a victory against Swedish society when the state's monopoly on violence cannot be upheld. As the morning paper *Svenska Dagbladet* commented:

> Rasmus Paludan is no more than the spark that made a pre-existing gunpowder keg explode. When he has gone back to Denmark, we will still have to live with this powder keg, which Swedish governments on the right and left have been filling up for decades, while dismissing it as a "challenge." This powder keg is now such that it takes no more than a well-directed spark for large numbers of young men to be prepared to try to kill Swedish police officers, or passengers on a bus in Malmö.[4]

## A Scary Society

In his book *Gangster Violence* (Sw. *Gangstervåld*), published in 2020, the police officer and criminologist Fredrik Kärrholm tells a journalist, in passing, about the six months he spent in Akalla (a residential area northwest of Stockholm). He didn't put his real name on the door, and when some young men outside the gate asked what he was doing there, he didn't say he was a policeman, but that he worked at the Tax Agency.

---

4   https://www.svd.se/a/z7Jb91/paskkravallerna-blottar-det-svenska-tillstandet.

"You didn't feel safe?," asked the journalist. He replied, "It wasn't about that, it was about minimising the risks," implying, "This is an area where it can be dangerous for an ethnic Swede to live, and if I had told them I was a policeman it could have been really dangerous."

When it comes to gang crime and riots in so-called deprived suburbs, how long can we afford to hold on to civilised, modern principles of individual autonomy and personal responsibility? When will the social climate become so harsh and the antagonisms so deep that we simply begin to see all non-Western immigrants as "the enemy," i.e. in the same way that many of them see "the Swedes" (Sw. *Svennarna*).

Imagine the future as Sweden now, but "more of the same." For people in general, Sweden will be more dangerous and poorer — hence worse. For a thinning bourgeoisie, Sweden will be materially better and safer — in gated communities. Behind walls and entrances protected by armed guards many of them will continue to celebrate the "open society." Even when they have other political preferences, the left-liberal political media complex rules their world of thought.

There is an even scarier alternative: Sweden has reached a stage where immigration-related societal problems have grown so large that they can no longer be dealt with within the usual "civilised" framework. In a decade or so, we may have civil war-like conditions in Sweden.

# OTHER BOOKS PUBLISHED BY ARKTOS

| | |
|---|---|
| Virginia Abernethy | *Born Abroad* |
| Sri Dharma Pravartaka Acharya | *The Dharma Manifesto* |
| Joakim Andersen | *Rising from the Ruins* |
| Winston C. Banks | *Excessive Immigration* |
| Stephen Baskerville | *Who Lost America?* |
| Alfred Baeumler | *Nietzsche: Philosopher and Politician* |
| Matt Battaglioli | *The Consequences of Equality* |
| Alain de Benoist | *Beyond Human Rights* |
| | *Carl Schmitt Today* |
| | *The Ideology of Sameness* |
| | *The Indo-Europeans* |
| | *Manifesto for a European Renaissance* |
| | *On the Brink of the Abyss* |
| | *The Problem of Democracy* |
| | *Runes and the Origins of Writing* |
| | *View from the Right* (vol. 1–3) |
| Armand Berger | *Tolkien, Europe, and Tradition* |
| Pawel Bielawski | *European Apostasy* |
| Arthur Moeller van den Bruck | *Germany's Third Empire* |
| Kerry Bolton | *The Perversion of Normality* |
| | *Revolution from Above* |
| | *Yockey: A Fascist Odyssey* |
| Isac Boman | *Money Power* |
| Daniel Branco | *The Absolute Philosopher* |
| Charles William Dailey | *The Serpent Symbol in Tradition* |
| Antoine Dresse | *Political Realism* |
| Ricardo Duchesne | *Faustian Man in a Multicultural Age* |
| Alexander Dugin | *Ethnos and Society* |
| | *Ethnosociology* |
| | *Eurasian Mission* |
| | *The Fourth Political Theory* |
| | *The Great Awakening vs the Great Reset* |
| | *Last War of the World-Island* |
| | *Politica Aeterna* |
| | *Political Platonism* |
| | *Putin vs Putin* |
| | *The Rise of the Fourth Political Theory* |
| | *The Trump Revolution* |
| | *Templars of the Proletariat* |
| | *The Theory of a Multipolar World* |
| Daria Dugina | *A Theory of Europe* |
| Edward Dutton | *Race Differences in Ethnocentrism* |
| Mark Dyal | *Hated and Proud* |
| Clare Ellis | *The Blackening of Europe* (vol. 1–3) |
| Koenraad Elst | *Return of the Swastika* |
| Julius Evola | *The Bow and the Club* |
| | *Fascism Viewed from the Right* |
| | *A Handbook for Right-Wing Youth* |
| | *Metaphysics of Power* |
| | *Metaphysics of War* |
| | *The Myth of the Blood* |

# OTHER BOOKS PUBLISHED BY ARKTOS

|  |  |
|---|---|
|  | *Notes on the Third Reich* |
|  | *Pagan Imperialism* |
|  | *Recognitions* |
|  | *A Traditionalist Confronts Fascism* |
| GUILLAUME FAYE | *Archeofuturism* |
|  | *Archeofuturism 2.0* |
|  | *The Colonisation of Europe* |
|  | *Convergence of Catastrophes* |
|  | *Ethnic Apocalypse* |
|  | *A Global Coup* |
|  | *Prelude to War* |
|  | *Sex and Deviance* |
|  | *Understanding Islam* |
|  | *Why We Fight* |
| DANIEL S. FORREST | *Suprahumanism* |
| ANDREW FRASER | *Dissident Dispatches* |
|  | *Reinventing Aristocracy in the Age of Woke Capital* |
|  | *The WASP Question* |
| GÉNÉRATION IDENTITAIRE | *We are Generation Identity* |
| PETER GOODCHILD | *The Taxi Driver from Baghdad* |
|  | *The Western Path* |
| PAUL GOTTFRIED | *War and Democracy* |
| GEORGES GUISCARD | *White Privilege* |
| PETR HAMPL | *Breached Enclosure* |
| PORUS HOMI HAVEWALA | *The Saga of the Aryan Race* |
| CONSTANTIN VON HOFFMEISTER | *Esoteric Trumpism* |
|  | *MULTIPOLARITY!* |
| RICHARD HOUCK | *Liberalism Unmasked* |
| A. J. ILLINGWORTH | *Political Justice* |
| INSTITUT ILIADE | *For a European Awakening* |
|  | *Guardians of Heritage* |
| ALEXANDER JACOB | *De Naturae Natura* |
| JASON REZA JORJANI | *Artemis Unveiled* |
|  | *Closer Encounters* |
|  | *Erosophia* |
|  | *Faustian Futurist* |
|  | *Iranian Leviathan* |
|  | *Lovers of Sophia* |
|  | *Metapolemos* |
|  | *Novel Folklore* |
|  | *Philosophy of the Future* |
|  | *Prometheism* |
|  | *Promethean Pirate* |
|  | *Prometheus and Atlas* |
|  | *Psychotron* |
|  | *Thanosis* |
|  | *Uber Man* |
|  | *World State of Emergency* |
| HENRIK JONASSON | *Sigmund* |
| EDGAR JULIUS JUNG | *The Significance of the German Revolution* |
| RUUBEN KAALEP & AUGUST MEISTER | *Rebirth of Europe* |
| LANCE KENNEDY | *The Book of the Scribe* |

# OTHER BOOKS PUBLISHED BY ARKTOS

# OTHER BOOKS PUBLISHED BY ARKTOS

| | |
|---|---|
| NICHOLAS ROONEY | *Talking to the Wolf* |
| RICHARD RUDGLEY | *Barbarians* |
| | *Essential Substances* |
| | *Wildest Dreams* |
| ERNST VON SALOMON | *It Cannot Be Stormed* |
| | *The Outlaws* |
| WERNER SOMBART | *Traders and Heroes* |
| PIERO SAN GIORGIO | *Giuseppe* |
| | *Survive the Economic Collapse* |
| | *Surviving the Next Catastrophe* |
| SRI SRI RAVI SHANKAR | *Celebrating Silence* |
| | *Know Your Child* |
| | *Management Mantras* |
| | *Patanjali Yoga Sutras* |
| | *Secrets of Relationships* |
| OSWALD SPENGLER | *The Decline of the West* |
| | *Man and Technics* |
| RICHARD STOREY | *The Uniqueness of Western Law* |
| J. R. SOMMER | *The New Colossus* |
| TOMISLAV SUNIC | *Against Democracy and Equality* |
| | *Homo Americanus* |
| | *Postmortem Report* |
| | *Titans are in Town* |
| ASKR SVARTE | *Gods in the Abyss* |
| HANS-JÜRGEN SYBERBERG | *On the Fortunes and Misfortunes of Art in Post-War Germany* |
| ABIR TAHA | *Defining Terrorism* |
| | *The Epic of Arya* (2nd ed.) |
| | *Nietzsche is Coming God, or the Redemption of the Divine* |
| | *Verses of Light* |
| JEAN THIRIART | *Europe: An Empire of 400 Million* |
| BAL GANGADHAR TILAK | *The Arctic Home in the Vedas* |
| BOSTIAN MARCO TURK | *War in the Name of Peace* |
| DOMINIQUE VENNER | *Ernst Jünger: A Different European Destiny* |
| | *For a Positive Critique* |
| | *The Shock of History* |
| HANS VOGEL | *How Europe Became American* |
| TIM VORGENS | *Legitimate Preference* |
| MARKUS WILLINGER | *A Europe of Nations* |
| | *Generation Identity* |
| ALEXANDER WOLFHEZE | *Alba Rosa* |
| | *Globus Horribilis* |
| | *Rupes Nigra* |

www.ingramcontent.com/pod-product-compliance
Lightning Source LLC
Chambersburg PA
CBHW031428270326
41930CB00007B/613